Legal Specialization

A HANDBOOK

Robert H. Edmunds, Jr.
EDITOR AND AUTHOR

AMERICAN BAR ASSOCIATION
Judicial Division

Cover design by Jill Tedhams/ABA Design

Printed in the United States of America.

29 28 27 26 25 5 4 3 2 1

A catalog record for this book is available from the Library of Congress.

Contents

About the Authors

Terry Ackerman earned his Ph.D. from the University of Wisconsin–Milwaukee in 1984. He has served as a psychometrician and held the E.F. Linquist Chair at the American College Testing (ACT) program. For over 30 years, he has taught graduate statistics and educational and psychological testing at the University of Illinois at Champaign-Urbana, the University of North Carolina at Greensboro, and the University of Iowa in Iowa City.

Dr. Ackerman has contributed his expertise to several technical advisory committees and consulted for companies like the Educational Testing Service, the College Board, the American Institute of Certified Public Accountants, and the Law School Admissions Council. He also chaired the Defense Advisory Committee, which oversees the Armed Services Vocational Aptitude Battery (ASVAB) testing for the U.S. military.

In addition, Dr. Ackerman has served as president of the National Council on Measurement in Education and the Psychometric Society, both international organizations dedicated to advancing educational and psychological measurement. He has also consulted with the North Carolina State Bar in developing and maintaining their legal specialty examinations and the paralegal certification examination.

Carolyn Dubay is secretary to the federal judiciary's Standing Committee on Rules of Practice and Procedure and Chief Counsel in the Rules Committee Office of the Office of General Counsel in the Administrative Office of the U.S. Courts. Prior to taking that position, she served as Deputy Judicial Officer in the Office of Judicial Integrity at the Administrative Office of the U.S. Courts. Before beginning work with the Administrative Office, Ms. Dubay served for over six years as the Executive Director of the North Carolina Judicial Standards Commission, the state's judicial disciplinary and ethics advisory agency, and served on the board of the national Association of Judicial Disciplinary Counsel. She is also an active member of the ABA Judicial Division and currently serves on the Ethics and Professionalism Committee. She is also a past chair of the Lawyers Conference of the Judicial Division, past chair of the Model Law Clerk Code of Conduct Working Group, and past chair of the Judicial Division's Programs Committee. Ms. Dubay's federal judicial service includes two years as a law clerk for the Honorable Joanna Seybert in the U.S. District Court for the Eastern District of New York and later work as an attorney-advisor at the Administrative Office and a senior researcher at the Federal Judicial Center. From 2007 to 2008, Ms. Dubay had the privilege of serving as a Supreme Court Fellow in the Office of the Counselor to the Chief Justice of the United States. She also practiced law as a civil litigator in North Carolina and Virginia with the firm Hunton & Williams. Ms. Dubay received her undergraduate degree in history from Duke University and her J.D. from Fordham University School of Law, where she served as an editor of the *Fordham Law Review* and graduated with honors. Ms. Dubay also received an L.L.M. with distinction from Georgetown University Law Center with a focus on international and comparative law.

Robert H. Edmunds, Jr. graduated from the University of North Carolina School of Law. Following service in the U.S. Navy as a line officer, he began work as an assistant district attorney. He later became an Assistant U.S. Attorney for the Middle District of North Carolina, then was appointed U.S. Attorney for that district by President Ronald Reagan. After leaving that position in 1993, he was a partner with the Greensboro, N.C., firm of Stern & Klepfer. While there, he was board certified as a specialist in state and federal criminal law in 1993 and as a specialist in appellate practice in 1994. In 1998, he was elected to the North Carolina Court of Appeals and in 2000 was elected to the Supreme Court of North Carolina, a position he held through two terms.

After leaving the Supreme Court, Mr. Edmunds became counsel at the firm of Fox Rothschild, LLP, practicing appellate law. In 2024, he was named Jurist in Residence at High Point University School of Law, where he teaches legal writing and criminal law while maintaining his practice with Fox Rothschild.

Denise E. Mullen received her Bachelor of Arts degree in psychology with a minor in sociology from Indiana University in Bloomington. She went on to receive a Master of Education from Kent State University in higher education administration. She worked at Cleveland State University and Case Western Reserve University before moving to North Carolina to work at Duke University as a Development Officer. She joined the staff at the North Carolina State Bar to coordinate the certification program for the Board of Legal Specialization in 2002. Dr. Mullen subsequently worked as Managing Director and retired after 22 years of service. She completed her doctorate in educational leadership and organizational innovation at Marymount University in March 2025.

Dr. Mullen has extensive program management experience, including wide-ranging capabilities with training and assessments for measuring effectiveness. She planned and directed numerous training programs for professionals who served on the certification committees as subject matter experts, writing and updating a training manual for their education and support. During her tenure, Dr. Mullen worked with hundreds of subject matter experts to write and grade specialty examinations, including creating and administering exam modules both in person and through remote online proctoring.

As a member of the state bar's Leadership/Management Planning Team, she developed and presented educational modules on leadership training for staff members as well. Dr. Mullen views herself as a facilitator/educator, focusing on encouraging others to recognize and value their own strengths while assessing the situation to determine the best leadership approaches to employ.

Grant B. Osborne is a North Carolina State Bar board-certified specialist in employment law, providing strategic counsel to employers across diverse industries on a broad range of workplace matters, such as regulatory compliance, wage and hour disputes, covenants not to compete, and labor relations. He also works with physicians and executives regarding employment agreements. With extensive experience representing clients in state and federal courts, Mr. Osborne also defends employers before key administrative agencies, including the Equal Employment Opportunity Commission, the National Labor Relations Board, and various wage and hour enforcement bodies. His practice also includes representation of employers in collective bargaining negotiations, handling union-related matters, and guiding employers through complex workplace investigations and litigation.

Beyond his legal advocacy, Mr. Osborne is a recognized leader in shaping employment law specialization in North Carolina. As chair of the Employment Law Specialty Committee for the North Carolina State Bar Board of Legal Specialization, he played a pivotal role in establishing employment law as a distinct board-certified specialty—an effort that required years of dedication, coordination with legal professionals, and the development of rigorous certification criteria. His leadership helped bring the initiative to fruition, culminating in the launch of the first certification exam for employment law specialists in the state.

Mr. Osborne is a proud alumnus of Duke University and the Duke University School of Law. His depth of knowledge, combined with a pragmatic and business-focused approach, makes him a trusted advisor for employers navigating the complexities of workplace law.

Troy D. Shelton is an appellate partner at Dowling PLLC in Raleigh, North Carolina. He has been certified as an appellate specialist by the North Carolina State Bar.

Mr. Shelton has a wide-ranging appellate practice. He has represented numerous elected officials, large corporations, and individuals in appeals. Mr. Shelton serves clients and trial attorneys in need of appellate representation in state and federal courts across the country. Besides regular appellate work, Mr. Shelton files amicus briefs in the appellate courts and appears in trial courts to assist trial attorneys on critical legal issues.

Mr. Shelton has been recognized for the quality of his appellate advocacy and for giving back to the profession. In 2024, Mr. Shelton was voted by his peers as the state's top appellate attorney, according to *Business North Carolina*. He was also recognized with the North Carolina Bar Association's top award in 2023 for pro bono service.

Introduction

Doctors have shown us the way. For almost every part of the human body, and for almost every disease, a medical specialization has been recognized. Lawyers have noticed and are following suit. A number of states have approved the process of board certification in specified areas of practice. Others should follow.

The benefits of specialization are twofold. First, the public is well served when those who need legal assistance in defined and/or complex areas of law can readily identify those practitioners most capable of providing that assistance. Second, board certification is an objective process based on experience, peer review, and testing. Being able to hold oneself out as a proven specialist is a powerful marketing tool.

This book is intended for two audiences. One audience is those attorneys who are interested in initiating a board certification process in a jurisdiction that does not now have one. The other audience is practitioners who are considering seeking the title of specialist for themselves. Both audiences can find value in the following chapters. For the first audience, the process of setting up a program ab initio is time-consuming at best and challenging when opposition arises. Yet the rewards can be great, as the contributors to this book have found. For the second audience, insights into the process should assist in achieving their goals.

Although it's been said that attorneys are a hundred percent for progress and a thousand percent against change, legal specialization is here to stay and will continue to grow. Just as medicine will always have general practitioners, law will always have its generalists. But as society continues its march toward ever-greater complexity, legal specialists will thrive. Join them!

Robert H. Edmunds, Jr.

Chapter 1

Specialization: A Creation Story

Robert H. Edmunds, Jr.

Apologia: The following chapter reads like an autobiography where "I" may be the most common word you see. Please be patient. While even I don't find my life all that fascinating, my experiences in this area are set out so that readers of this book can see both the value of board certification and the efforts it takes to establish and maintain a viable program, while perhaps picking up some useful suggestions.

I had the good fortune to begin my legal career as an assistant district attorney, prosecuting state criminal cases at all levels from traffic court to career criminals. As a result, I was in court on a daily basis. The only drawback was that appeals to the North Carolina appellate division were handled by the state's attorney general. After a trial, the prosecutor heard nothing more about the case until an opinion was issued. It irked me that I was unable to follow through with the prosecutions I handled, especially when the conviction was reversed. As the trial attorney, I knew a lot more about the case than the assistant attorney general, who was only reading a transcript.

The situation improved when I was hired as an assistant U.S. attorney for the Middle District of North Carolina, prosecuting federal cases. Not only were prosecutors expected to brief and argue the appeals of cases they handled, but I also found that I enjoyed appellate work. In addition, more than one appeal was saved when I was able to answer questions posed by the appellate bench about why the case had been treated a particular way. As the one who had been in the arena (to steal a phrase from Teddy Roosevelt), I could explain both strategic and tactical decisions and respond to questions about what had happened in the courtroom. For example, take a look at *United States v. Pitino*, 887 F.2d 42 (1989), where I was able to explain a gap in the written plea agreement.

Following several years as an assistant U.S. attorney, I was appointed U.S. attorney for the district. The upshot was that I was now able to assign especially interesting cases to myself. During my tenure, I tried (usually in tandem with one of the office's assistant U.S. attorneys) cases involving such crimes as international drug smuggling and public corruption. And every conviction was followed by an appeal.

However, when I left the U.S. attorney's office and entered private practice as a criminal defense attorney, I found myself starting from scratch. As I struggled to build a client base, I noticed an advertisement in *North Carolina Lawyers Weekly*, the newspaper for state practitioners. The ad both reminded attorneys of the North Carolina State Bar's specialization program, which then had been in existence for only a few years, and encouraged them to consider applying for board certification as a specialist.[1]

The timing was perfect. I could not think of a better way both to use the experience I had gained over the years and to attract clients than to go through the objective process of being board certified. Under the state program, an attorney can be certified in no more than two fields. I requested an application to be

1. The North Carolina State Bar is a state agency to which all attorneys licensed in the state must belong. It regulates the legal profession and, pertinent to this book, manages the attorney board certification program. The North Carolina Bar Association is a voluntary attorney organization that addresses various needs of the legal profession.

certified in state and federal criminal law (treated as one field) and another application to be certified in criminal appellate practice.

To say that the applications were daunting would be a substantial understatement. In addition to questions regarding applicable continuing legal education courses recently attended, the nature of the applicant's practice, any bar discipline, peer references, and so on, the application required detailed information about substantial involvement in the field.

For the criminal law application, the first substantial involvement question related to my entire career. I was required to provide information about five felonies submitted as counsel of record to juries for decision, ten additional felony or misdemeanor trials submitted to juries for decision, fifty other criminal matters tried to disposition in state or federal courts, two state or federal appeals in which I had presented the oral argument, and three state or federal appeals in which I had the primary responsibility for preparing the record on appeal and the brief. A second set of questions related to the previous five years. I had to affirm that, over that period, I had participated in one or more criminal jury trials for at least 25 days, had made 75 court appearances in substantive nonjury trials or proceedings, and had devoted an average of 500 hours per year (and not less than 400 hours in any one year) to the practice of criminal law. Holy cow!

The criminal appellate practice application mercifully repeated many of the same questions regarding criminal trial work over both my career and the last five years. However, relating specifically to criminal appellate experience, it required a list of 15 such appeals I had handled over my career, including five within the past two years. In addition, I had to submit copies of the briefs I had filed in my two most recent appeals.

Rummaging through old files and digging out detailed information relating to 75 criminal trials and 15 criminal appeals was a daunting task involving lots of dust and sneezing. What struck me most forcibly, though, was how few attorneys would be able to meet these minimum requirements even to apply for board certification in these fields. Those most likely to be eligible were state and federal prosecutors and public defenders who had a steady load of cases, but they were government employees with little incentive to seek certification. I was fortunate in that my recent departure from the U.S. Department of Justice meant that a number of cases I had tried and/or handled on appeal while U.S. attorney fell within the five-year deadline set out in both applications.

Of course, the application was only the beginning. My application to take the criminal law examination was accepted, but the application to take the criminal appellate examination was denied because no applicable CLE had been offered in the preceding 12 months. Fortunately, the Board of Legal Specialization allowed the application to extend to the following year, so I was able to take that examination later without reapplying. This glitch points out one of the better aspects of the process. While the requirements to take the examinations are demanding, an applicant who has fallen short in a particular area could ask for a waiver from the board. Waivers were not routinely granted, but an applicant who was stymied by unusual circumstances had a reasonable chance of obtaining relief.

The written examinations were tough, and by the time each was over, I wondered why I'd deviated from the vow I made after graduating from law school and passing the bar never, ever to take another exam. But the news was good from both, and I was board certified as a specialist in state and federal criminal law and, the following year, board certified as a specialist in criminal appellate practice.

Numerous benefits followed. The North Carolina State Bar issued annual directories of board-certified specialists in all fields. As the internet matured, the directory was also made available online. The State Bar held annual meetings of specialists so that we could get to know each other and create networks for referrals. The state's ethics rules allowed specialists to note their fields of expertise on office stationery, business cards, and so on. Appointments by state and federal courts to handle criminal trials and appeals increased. The ability to promote myself as a board-certified specialist helped me develop my client base while also benefiting the firm in which I was a partner.

The board certification proved its worth in another way when I tiptoed into state politics. In 1996, I was recruited to run for the office of attorney general of North Carolina. Though I'd given little thought to politics, my experience as U.S. attorney persuaded me that I could handle the job if elected. Unfortunately (at least in the short term), I ran against a popular incumbent who trounced me.[2]

Nevertheless, during that race I was treated as a serious candidate due in no small part to my board certification. And so, when the opportunity arrived to run for the North Carolina Court of Appeals two years later, the board certification as an appellate specialist was a definite asset. Although each of the candidates claimed to be the best qualified, I could legitimately point out that I was the only one who had gone through the rigorous process of certification and had a piece of paper from the North Carolina State Bar attesting that I was a specialist in the legal field of criminal appellate practice. Just as a heart patient will seek a physician who is a board-certified thoracic surgeon or cardiologist and has proven that he or she knows the surgical theater, I could show that I was a capable appellate practitioner.

In short, the board certification allowed me to stand out from the other candidates and was cited by many who made endorsements. The voters noticed. Then two years after my election to

---

2. As an aside, though the incumbent and I were not much more than acquaintances at the time of that election, we have since become good buddies—not all politics is poisonous.

the Court of Appeals, I was encouraged to run for a seat on the Supreme Court of North Carolina. Once again, the board certification proved its value as I was elected to the state's high court.

Meanwhile, during the years of private practice following my departure from federal practice, I'd been involved with the North Carolina Bar Association's Appellate Rules Committee.[3] This Committee consists of volunteer attorneys and appellate judges who, in coordination with the appellate judiciary, work with the state's rules of appellate procedure to make them more user-friendly both for appellate courts and for appellate practitioners. Although this Committee addressed the North Carolina rules, many members also handled federal appeals and were familiar with the Federal Rules of Appellate Procedure. In fact, that Committee several times successfully recommended to the Supreme Court of North Carolina that it adopt state appellate rule modifications to mirror a more effective federal procedure.

When I first joined the Appellate Rules Committee, it seemed to be a sleepy backwater of the North Carolina Bar Association, peopled mostly by a small but intense cadre of practitioners who basked in that sort of thing. Over time, though, the Appellate Rules Committee became a hot ticket. Perennial members became judges, justices, the state's solicitor general, clerks of the appellate courts, and so on. Young judicial elbow clerks who aspired to practice appellate law joined, as did practitioners who

---

3. Two "committees" are involved in this saga. To avoid both confusion and tedious repetition, I will refer to the Appellate Rules Committee of the North Carolina Bar Association as the "Committee" (with a capital "C") and the appellate specialization committee of the North Carolina State Bar as the "committee" or the "specialization committee" (with a small "c"). As detailed in this chapter, the former Committee deals with the state's Rules of Appellate Procedure, while the latter committee is responsible for setting up an area of specialization for approval by the State Bar, then preparing and administering examinations for those who seek certification as a specialist in that field. There was, and is, much overlap in the membership of the Committee and the committee.

found value in off-the-record interactions with the judiciary and opportunities to work together on subcommittees. The North Carolina Bar Association had to schedule the Committee's meetings for increasingly large rooms.

Even so, it struck me that the Appellate Rules Committee was missing a beat. Though it was packed to the gunwales with attorneys and judicial officials who demonstrated at every meeting their devotion to the improvement of appellate practice, I was the only member who was a board-certified specialist in the field. In fact, if memory serves, the state boasted only about five board-certified specialists in criminal appellate practice when I took the exam. While the test was administered sporadically over the following years, there were few takers. By the time I became a justice, there were seven living specialists in that field, and some of them had left practice for the trial bench.

So at nearly every meeting of the Committee, when the chair called for new business, I would put my hand up and say that we ought to take steps to reinvigorate the specialization in criminal appellate practice. The result was always the same, one that I believe is familiar to judges around the world: other members would nod thoughtfully and say that it was an excellent idea. Then the conversation would move on to the next agenda item.

Eventually, I took a deep breath one day, called the North Carolina State Bar, asked for the director of the specialization program, and spoke with Alice Mine (now the recently retired Executive Director of the State Bar and predecessor of coauthor Denise Mullen). When I explained to Ms. Mine the purpose of the call, she was more than happy to describe the steps that would be needed. First, I needed to read the applicable statutes to determine the minimum requirements for the certification set by the General Assembly. Second, she advised that, even though the criminal appellate specialization was in existence, it would be necessary effectively to start from scratch because it had become moribund. She warned that things would get complicated.

The North Carolina State Bar's overarching Board of Legal Specialization is responsible for managing all the recognized areas of specialization. Anyone seeking to establish a new (or rejuvenated) area of specialization needed to present a proposal to that board and earn its approval. The proposal required inclusion of a formal definition of the practice area, the signatures of 100 attorneys recommending the creation of the new specialty area, a demonstration that the proposal addressed an established practice area, signatures of 20 lawyers who would be interested in seeking certification in the proposed practice area, signatures of ten lawyers who would be willing to serve on the initial specialization committee that would draft standards for the proposed specialty, and a list of continuing legal education programs offered in the area, plus other odds and ends. Whew. Alice Mine was right; this was going to be a slog. Fortunately, the personnel at the State Bar responsible for the specialization programs were eager to help.

And so the journey began. Very early in the process, the State Bar realized that the talent pool would be a lot deeper if the specialization were broadened to include both civil and criminal appeals. The effect would be to shelve our plans to reinvigorate the criminal appellate specialization and begin anew with a more general Appellate Practice specialization. Those who were currently certified in criminal appellate practice would be (to their delight) grandfathered into the new specialization.

My first job was to recruit at least ten attorneys to serve on the appellate committee that would draft standards for the appellate specialization. The State Bar further let me know that, assuming standards were successfully drafted and the specialization proposal approved, the members of that initial specialization committee would be expected to serve at least long enough to draft and grade the first examination. In other words, an attorney accepting an invitation to join the specialization committee would be agreeing to commit substantial volunteer time to the project. Their reward was that each would be designated an appellate specialist without having to take the exam.

Having seen many appellate practitioners both from my perch on the bench and from my participation in the North Carolina Bar Association's Appellate Rules Committee, I had some ideas about the new specialization committee's membership. The State Bar's practices required that the specialization committee be diverse in a number of ways, including geographically. That last standard was the toughest because most of the specialization committee work would be done in Raleigh, the state capital, while the boundaries of the state are hours away by car—this in the days before COVID and widespread familiarity with remote meeting programs. I looked for practitioners who I knew both represented their clients effectively on appeal and gave the appellate courts well-researched and well-argued briefs, as well as candidates in the offices of the attorney general and the state appellate defender.

When I began calling around, I was pleased to find not only that lawyers are reluctant to say "no" to a Supreme Court justice, but also that most were pleased to be asked and genuinely enthusiastic about the prospect of the specialization. Signing them up was easy. Ms. Mine and I also explored the idea of increasing the attractiveness of the appellate specialization by establishing a rump advisory committee that would consist entirely of retired chief justices of the Supreme Court of North Carolina. Once the State Bar approved awarding the specialization status to each of the participating former chiefs without their having to take the exam, every one signed up. None took much persuading.

The State Bar staff helped us formulate a formal definition of the proposed practice area, which would include both state and federal appeals. With that, I appeared before the State Bar's Board of Legal Specialization to discuss the proposed appellate specialization and seek its approval to proceed. Fortunately, that board was receptive and, as far as I could tell, did not need to be sold on the potential value of this specialization. Their blessing was forthcoming.

So far, so good. The remaining steps were more challenging. The "substantial involvement" (described earlier) required for an applicant to sit for the examination was a major stumbling block. As that term was defined at the time, very few practitioners outside of government practice had the concentrated and consistent experience necessary even to fill out the application. Yet the applicable statute required that an applicant be able to prove substantial involvement in some legitimate form. So the question was whether "substantial involvement" could be redefined to encompass a larger universe of potential applicants while still preserving the underlying requirement that the applicant have demonstrated expertise in the field.

The folks at the North Carolina State Bar were aware of this difficulty, and we all brainstormed alternatives. Could participation in a moot court count as a court appearance? We decided that the answer was "no." While a moot court can be harrowing, nothing real is on the line, particularly not the fate of a living, breathing client. Could the required number of arguments be adjusted? This question particularly resonated because the North Carolina Court of Appeals was reducing the number of appeals in which it heard oral argument, instead deciding an increasing number on the basis of the briefs alone. The State Bar was willing to work with the appellate specialization committee to redefine the required number of oral arguments.[4] Another question was what about an attorney's participation as second chair? We all

4. Incidentally, this issue led to another. Attorneys are permitted to ask the North Carolina Court of Appeals to allow oral argument in a particular case. Is it ethical to make such a request to beef up the attorney's number of arguments if the attorney cannot affirm that oral argument will benefit the client? See Carolyn Dubay's contribution to this book (Chapter 4).

know that, quite often, the original research and initial drafting of an appellate brief is undertaken by an associate or junior partner, while the first name on the final product is that of a senior partner, who also makes the oral argument. We were able to tweak the requirements to allow credit for work on a brief and partial participation in an argument. Do amicus briefs count? What about judicial clerks, who see lots of trials and work on opinions and orders? What about law professors who teach appellate practice but do not practice what they teach? What about sitting appellate judges and justices, who enforce the rules of appellate procedure but neither prepare records and briefs nor make oral arguments?

The questions seem unending, and I'll note that this tension between the requirement of "substantial involvement," the reality that oral arguments are increasingly rare, and applicants' reasonable requests for a finding that they have demonstrated "substantial involvement" is being played out to this day. I am happy to report, though, that the appellate specialization committee was able to work with the State Bar to the extent that, the first year the exam was administered after the appellate specialization was approved, a solid cadre of applicants was able successfully to apply to stand for the exam.

We also addressed issues common to all specialization programs. Some attorneys who readily can meet the requirements are unwilling to participate or are not interested for any number of reasons. Some are reluctant to take an examination they might fail, while others have a thriving practice and see no need for the certification. These were, and are, marketing issues that I expect all similar specialization programs face. Fortunately, at least in my experience, success breeds success so that, over time, certification becomes the norm in many areas of practice. I discuss later some of the steps taken by the North Carolina State Bar, the North Carolina Bar Association, and the specialization committee to make the process attractive to potential applicants.

The appellate specialization committee's next task was to prepare the examination. Again, the State Bar provided critical assistance in the form of Dr. Terry Ackerman, who was then a professor in the Education Department at the University of North Carolina at Greensboro. Dr. Ackerman, who contributed Chapter 3 of this book, had been working with other specialization committees of the State Bar. During a series of meetings, and with the help of Dr. Ackerman, the appellate specialization committee prepared its exam.

At the beginning of the process, Dr. Ackerman pointed out to us that the format of the examination could be determined by the nature of the legal practice being scrutinized. For instance, the examination for specialization in bankruptcy law had little in common with the examination for specialization in family law. Instead, he impressed upon us the importance of drafting examination questions that could be graded objectively, of setting appropriate cut scores (which determine the difference between a satisfactory and an unsatisfactory answer), and, most importantly, of creating an examination that tested those qualities that most define competency in our field.

The specialization committee considered a number of alternatives. Should the exam be open-book? We concluded that no sane appellate attorney works without constantly referring to the Rules of Appellate Procedure or other sources—reliance on memory is the royal road to malpractice—and that applicants would be permitted to access certain materials. What about the format of the questions? Some specialization examinations consisted of nothing but short-answer questions, while others focused on essays.

We ultimately concluded that the exam would have to include several parts in order to test all of an applicant's skills. The first part would be multiple-choice. Dr. Ackerman gave the specialization committee guidance in drafting valid questions and answers along with legitimate distractors that sounded plausible but were wrong. A second part would consist of longer questions or scenarios seeking short essay responses. Since the specialization covered a wide range of practices, we concluded that the fairest approach was to draft four questions and require the examinee to address three. The option of choosing which three to answer allowed an examinee who was wholly inexperienced in one area (for instance, federal appeals) to skip that question without penalty.

The third part of the examination would test writing skills. The specialization committee created a set of facts that described a scenario, a resulting trial that included several rulings by the trial court on motions made by counsel, a jury verdict, and a notice of appeal with an accompanying record. Part of a prewritten brief to an appellate court was given to the examinee. That part was deliberately loaded with errors ranging from trivial ("trail court" instead of "trial court") to significant (omission of a designation of the standard of review) that the examinee was required to identify. In accordance with Dr. Ackerman's instructions, each correctly identified error was given an appropriate point value.

The other portion of this third part of the exam required the examinee to draft an argument on an issue raised by the appeal. This portion of the examination would be a take-home so that the examinee could adequately research and polish their response within a deadline of approximately one week. The specialization committee realized that it would be necessary to limit the scope of the applicant's research, so the examination included a list of citations to applicable cases, rules, and other sources (both favorable and unfavorable) to which the examinee was limited in drafting their argument. Understanding how lawyers think, the specialization committee included specific warnings that citing additional or different sources was not allowed and would gain the applicant no additional points.

Grading this portion of the exam was demanding because the responses were all different, reflecting the writing style of the applicant and other subjective factors. To address this concern, the grading rubric for this portion of the exam identified for the grader a specified value for the issues that each applicant was expected to spot, address, and, if necessary, distinguish in a competent argument.

You have probably noticed that the exam did not include a moot court. The committee gave long and serious consideration to this issue—after all, the acme of appellate practice is making a compelling argument that persuades a panel to adopt your position—but we could not think of any way to structure a process that would control all the variables and allow the applicant to be graded objectively. We reluctantly dropped the idea.

Once the exam was drafted, the specialization committee discussed how to make the process of becoming certified attractive to the appellate bar. Historically, the North Carolina Bar Association's Appellate Rules Committee had presented an all-day CLE program on appellate practice every year or two. The specialization committee decided to use that CLE slot as a method for publicizing the new and improved specialization while at the same time encouraging practitioners to apply for the exam. The CLE, given a few months before that first examination, was titled "Gateway to Specialization" and was designed to teach to the test. For example, the CLE included a section addressing practice before the U.S. Supreme Court because the exam included a question about that Court.

Finally, I took advantage of my judicial position and "suggested" to my clerks that they take the exam as a final test of its validity. Their responses allowed the committee to remove some minor snags while giving us welcome assurance that the exam was reasonable.

I became a true believer in Dr. Ackerman's methods when the specialization committee graded the first set of examinations. He had stressed the importance of objectivity in the grading. Knowing that objectivity is hard to measure when grading essay-type answers, the procedure that the specialization committee followed was to give each anonymous examination to two members to grade with the understanding that, should the two graders reach inconsistent results on a particular exam or part of an exam, other graders would be called in. The graders all used the same rubrics in assigning scores. After each grader completed his or her work, the specialization committee met to compare results.

Those results were as impressive as they were gratifying. Even though each grader worked independently, they all arrived at scores that were consistently within one or two points of each other. In other words, the scores for each exam strongly converged, no matter who was grading it. Dr. Ackerman's process of creating and then grading the examination had excluded or at least effectively limited subjectivity on the part of the graders. I began to think that maybe I'd been wrong to assume for years that law school exam grades were based mostly on "the chancellor's foot."[5]

An additional step the specialization committee took following the examination was to review the multiple-choice questions to identify any that had been consistently answered incorrectly by the applicants. Such a result would indicate that the question and/or the answers were poorly drafted or deficient in some other way. Those questions would not be used again in future exams and, if the wrong answer to the bad question meant the difference between an applicant's passing and failing, the exam was regraded without considering that question.

Following the exam, the specialization committee reached out to those who had taken the exam for feedback. Was the exam too hard? Too easy? How did the applicants feel about having a take-home question? Was the option to choose among short essay questions helpful? Did the multiple-choice questions hit the sweet

---

5. https://www.lsd.law/define/chancellors-foot#:~:text=Chancellor's%20foot%20is%20a%20term,%2C%20a%2017th%2Dcentury%20jurist (last visited Mar. 18, 2025).

spot between being too nitpicking and too general? The specialization committee was pleased (and relieved) to find that the test-takers, those who failed as well as those who passed, reported that the examination was fair. The specialization committee has continued to employ this same format, and the responses received from those who have taken the exam over the years consistently have supported its use.

That's the saga of the appellate specialization to date. As I write, the 2024 exam has just been administered and graded. The number of board-certified specialists in appellate practice continues to grow in North Carolina.

While I hope that this recitation has been of some use to anyone considering instituting a specialization program, be mindful that my experience is not necessarily typical. In North Carolina, some areas of specialization attract far more applicants than the appellate specialization does, and the format of exams in other areas appropriately reflects the skills needed there. States that have specialization programs often administer them differently. In North Carolina, the General Assembly sets out statutory requirements for specialization, while the mandatory North Carolina State Bar administers it. In other states, the specialization programs are administered by the state's high court. Those hoping to create a specialization program in a state that has none have many models from which to choose.

Nevertheless, I believe that some universal truths can be gleaned. The presence and participation of the judiciary can be an enormous asset in bar projects. Lawyers like to hang out with judges, lawyers are flattered when asked to work with judges, and lawyers tend to say "yes" when asked by a judge to join the fun. If you are a judge, volunteer. If you are a practitioner considering starting a specialization program in your state or a new specialty area within an existing program, draft a judge or two. They can help you bulldoze your way through all sorts of potential obstacles.

Specialization brings like-minded attorneys together. Each field of specialization needs a cadre of attorneys who are willing to do the necessary scut work, such as preparing materials, drafting and grading examinations, coordinating with the administrative agency, recruiting other volunteers, promoting the specialization, and so on. These volunteers commit hours to the good of the practice without recompense (or billable hours), but their efforts are indispensable. You can be one.

Finally, and most importantly, the practice of law is enhanced by specialization. I frequently receive calls and emails from other lawyers, including those in my firm, asking for a "good lawyer" practicing in a particular field in some far-off town. I always look first in the State Bar's guide to see if there are any board-certified specialists in that area. If so, and even if I don't know the listed lawyer(s), I can respond by giving the contact information of the specialist along with the assurance that the specialist has proven that they are competent in that particular area of practice. Everyone benefits.

Chapter 2

Specialty Certification for Lawyers

Denise E. Mullen, M.Ed., Ed.D.

In some states, lawyers have been able to become board-certified specialists since the mid-1980s. Specialization programs were initially proposed as a way to promote legitimate competency among lawyers in the face of potentially misleading legal advertisements. By 1983, 12 states had adopted state-sponsored certification plans. About ten years later, the ABA adopted standards allowing private legal specialty groups to sponsor certification programs as well. Currently, 20 states and eight national organizations have functioning specialty certification programs for lawyers.

Here's what's involved in a specialization program, how to set one up if you don't have one, and ideas for improvement if you do.

Specialty Certification for Lawyers: Certificate or Certification?

In most cases, a certificate shows that an individual completed an educational course or program. Several law schools now offer graduate certificate programs for legal professionals who work in highly regulated fields. Earning this type of certificate is a one-time accomplishment. Board certification, in comparison, indicates that a lawyer has passed an examination covering specific practice area topics. In addition to passing an exam, board-certified lawyers must meet other minimum requirements, including filing an application for recertification every five years.

Excellence or Proficiency

One of the first things that will need to be decided when developing a specialization program is the standard for initial certification. Some programs set a standard of proficiency, while some set a standard of expertise. The North Carolina Board of Legal Specialization, for example, uses a standard of proficiency, based on acknowledging that certification does not necessitate expertise in the law of a specific specialty. Legal practice in any area often requires referring to resources such as statutes, regulations, and case law, which are accessible to attorneys in practice but not during a certification examination. The board also recognizes that the requirement of five years of substantial involvement suggests that the standard is not mastery, as achieving mastery in a legal specialty typically takes longer than five years. Therefore the standards emphasize "proficiency" and "competence" rather than the more advanced standard of "mastery."

Standards

The standards for initial certification address Licensure, Substantial Involvement, CLE, Peer Review, and Examination. Many state programs use the American Bar Association (ABA) Accreditation of Specialty Certification Programs for Lawyers Standards (or model rules) as a foundation for their own rules. Most national programs use the model rules as well.

The ABA defines minimum requirements as follows:

- "**Substantial Involvement:** Substantial involvement in the specialty area throughout the three-year period immediately preceding application to the certifying organization. Substantial involvement is measured by the type and number of cases or matters handled and the amount of time spent practicing in the specialty area and require that the time spent in practicing the specialty be no less than twenty-five percent (25%) of the total practice of a lawyer engaged in a normal full-time practice.

- **Peer Review:** A minimum of five references, a majority of which are from attorneys or judges who are knowledgeable regarding the practice area and are familiar with the competence of the lawyer, and none of which are from persons related to or engaged in legal practice with the lawyer.
- **Written Examination:** An evaluation of the lawyer's knowledge of the substantive and procedural law in the specialty area, determined by written examination of suitable length and complexity.
- **Educational Experience:** A minimum of 36 hours of participation in continuing legal education in the specialty area in the three-year period preceding the lawyer's application for certification.
- **Good Standing:** A lawyer seeking certification is admitted to practice and is a member in good standing in one or more states or territories of the United States or the District of Columbia."

Most state and national programs use the ABA minimum standards as a foundation, though many go beyond these requirements with additional standards, particularly in terms of hours of involvement and additional specifications on continuing legal education content or credits.

Governance Models

Options for governance of programs include state-sponsored and -administered programs, national certifying organizations, states that offer only certifications from ABA-accredited national organizations, and states that only permit lawyers certified by an ABA-accredited organization to communicate that status. A few states require disclaimer language, do not permit certification, or do not address certification in their governing rules.

State-Sponsored Programs

Some states offer and manage their own specialty certification programs. These are generally housed in the state bar or bar association or under the administration of a state supreme court. The governance model generally impacts how specialties are proposed, administered, and revised. Most state programs have clearly defined standards that regulate the program design and implementation.

Some of the national programs work with individual states to create joint-certification programs. For example, a lawyer can pursue certification in business bankruptcy law through the American Board of Certification and, with a passing exam score, become certified in North Carolina as well.

These states administer their own specialty certification programs: Arizona, California*, Connecticut*, Florida*, Indiana*, Louisiana*, Minnesota*, New Jersey, New Mexico, North Carolina, Ohio*, Pennsylvania*, South Carolina, and Texas*.

National Certifying Organizations

The national programs follow the ABA minimum standards and must receive ABA accreditation as well as follow procedures in some states for individual state accreditation. Some states allow ABA-accredited programs to function in the state with no additional application procedures required.

*Indicates states that also accredit/approve private certifiers.

Examples of national certifying organizations: The American Board of Certification, American Board of Professional Liability Attorneys, International Association for Privacy Professionals, National Association of Counsel for Children, National Association of Estate Planners & Councils, National Board of Trial Advocacy, National College of DUI Defense, Inc., and the National Elder Law Foundation.

States with Partnership Programs

Some states partner with national certification programs to allow lawyers to become certified specialists. For example, Tennessee recognizes 14 legal specialties for lawyers who have been certified by one of seven ABA-accredited programs. Tennessee does not issue a separate state certification.

States that accredit or approve private certifiers: Alabama, Idaho, Maine, Nevada, South Dakota, and Tennessee.

States That Permit Communication of Certification

These are states with ethical rules permitting certified lawyers to communicate information concerning certification if granted by an ABA-accredited organization and, in some cases, identified as such.

States that permit communication: Alaska, Arkansas, Delaware, District of Columbia, Georgia, Hawaii, Iowa, Kansas, Kentucky, Massachusetts, Mississippi, Montana, Nebraska, New Hampshire, New York, North Dakota, Utah, Virginia, Wisconsin, and Wyoming.

States with Disclaimers or Prohibitions

Some states generally allow lawyers to disclose their certification but require language indicating that the state does not certify specialists in any field.

States that require disclaimer language: Colorado, Illinois, Missouri, Oklahoma, Rhode Island, and Washington.

The states that prohibit disclosure or do not address certification are Maryland, Oregon, and West Virginia.

There are many options for offering board certification to lawyers and many options for lawyers to pursue becoming board-certified specialists.

Creating a New Specialty Certification

Application Process

One example of an application process for starting a new specialty area in an existing program is the North Carolina process. This application process for a new specialty area includes nine key components. These components were selected to demonstrate to the governing body that the practice area does require special skills and knowledge, that there is sufficient support among the bar to create the new specialty, and that enough lawyers are interested in pursuing the specialty to justify adding it to the program. These application requirements are:

1. Signatures of 100 lawyers recommending the creation of the proposed specialty area. (Lawyers do not have to qualify for or be interested in being certified in the practice area.)
2. A statement as to whether reputable professional organizations have an existing practice section or committee in the proposed specialty area and the current number of members in that section or committee.
3. A demonstration that it is an established practice area by providing information about one or more of the following:
   - Other states or accredited national organizations offering the specialty
   - Listing as practice area in Martindale Hubble

- Listing as practice area in Best Lawyers in America
- Referral service listings (local bar associations or other services)

4. Signatures of 20 lawyers who are interested in seeking certification in the proposed specialty area.
5. A definition of the proposed specialty area.
6. A statement that the contemplated definition of the proposed specialty area neither is in substantial conflict, nor substantially overlaps, with the definition of a current specialty area, or, if substantial conflict or overlap exists, a statement explaining why the proposed specialty area should be recognized in spite of the conflict or overlap.
7. An explanation about how recognition of the proposed specialty area will benefit members of the public.
8. A listing of the continuing legal education courses in the proposed specialty area provided during the previous two years by CLE sponsors accredited by State Bar (Association) Continuing Legal Education Departments.
9. Signatures of at least ten lawyers who would be willing to serve as members of the initial specialty committee that will draft standards for the proposed specialty.
10. Showing of support: The governing body will need to see a strong show of support in order to consider the creation of a new specialty practice area. Some practice areas are well established and likely to receive little negative commentary. Other practice area proposals may be more controversial and raise opposition among bar members. It is important to think through these possibilities and find ways to reach consensus if possible.
11. Feedback from lawyers and governance: When a board or governing body is considering the adoption of a new specialty area, the first step is to review the application and determine if all requirements have been met. Many states have a multi-step process that includes several necessary approvals. Comments and questions may be encountered

at any step and must be addressed before proceeding to the next step in the process. Robust discussion and consideration of alternate viewpoints may occur.

Levels of Approval

One example of the process includes:

1. Consideration by board of legal specialization—if approved at this level, the board will appoint an initial specialty committee to draft proposed standards.
2. Presentation of the proposed standards to the state bar's governing body. If approved at this level, the state bar will publish the proposal for comments throughout the next fiscal quarter.
3. Comments and questions received during the quarter will be distributed to the specialty committee for response or revision. If revisions are needed, the process returns to step two, and the proposed standards must be submitted to the state bar council for a second time.
4. If no revisions are needed, the proposed standards are presented to the state bar's governing body for final approval.
5. If approved by the state bar, the proposed standards are then submitted to the state supreme court for adoption.

Initial Specialty Committee

The initial specialty committee should be made up of a diverse group of legal professionals who represent different locations, practice types, and clients, as well as different genders and ethnic and racial backgrounds. This is an important step, as these committee members will be writing the exam questions and will need to be aware of any bias they potentially bring to the process. The goal is to create a valid and reliable exam that gives accurate results of qualification without giving any one group an unanticipated advantage.

Subject Matter Experts

These initial committee members will also serve as the subject matter experts (SMEs) who will write and grade the exams. Their personal experience and knowledge base will be important as decisions are made about exam design and content. SMEs will need to work collaboratively to determine the breadth and depth of knowledge necessary for applicants to attain certification.

In order to establish the specialty practice area early, it is best to have a wide reach for initial involvement in the committee. The benefit for the initial committee member SMEs is that they will be certified without having to take and pass an exam. The effort they put into drafting and administering the exam, however, can be quite time-consuming. These SMEs earn their certification with the knowledge and commitment required to create good exam questions, set the standard for a passing score (for more on standard setting, see Chapter 3), and grade the exams.

Program Management

Specialty Committees

Specialty committees are made up of seven members who are certified in the practice area. Committee members are appointed for up to two consecutive three-year terms. Terms are staggered so that institutional knowledge remains as committee members rotate on and off. Appointing both a committee chair and vice chair is strongly recommended to ensure that staff can communicate with the committee on a timely basis when needed.

Application Process

Applications for initial certification are typically accepted during an open application period once or twice a year, depending on the exam schedule offered. Initial applicants complete the required application form and submit any additional required documentation to demonstrate that they meet each of the requirements and are eligible to sit for the exam.

Applications for initial certification are first evaluated by a staff member to confirm that the application is complete and that all required documents have been submitted. The staff evaluation includes a review of licensure (including licensure in other states), a review of any disclosed disciplinary records, a review of substantial involvement, confirmation of the CLE record, and a review of any requests for waiver of strict compliance with the standards. Staff confirms that each of these components is sufficient for committee review and, if so, sends peer reference forms to be completed.

Once peer references have been received, staff compiles completed application packets for committee review. The specialty committees review all completed applications and make a recommendation to the board regarding each candidate's eligibility to sit for an exam.

Requests for Waiver of Strict Compliance

Candidates who do not meet a particular certification standard may request a waiver of strict compliance with that standard. Examples include a candidate who does not meet the CLE or substantial involvement requirement for one year due to a medical issue, parental leave, or active military service. Because these requests have become more frequent over the past few years, it is beneficial for a program to establish guidelines for the approval of these requests. One example is a policy that allows staff to approve waiver requests under certain circumstances. See the following policy example:

> A waiver of strict compliance with respect to the CLE requirements applicable to initial application for specialty certification shall be granted when the applicant

(a) has completed at least 80 percent of the total CLE hour requirement,

(b) is not deficient in more than one year of the application review period with respect to any specialty-specific minimum annual hour requirement relative to either specialty or related-topic CLE hours,

(c) has an average of specialty-specific CLE hours in the deficiency year and either the year immediately preceding or the year immediately succeeding the deficiency year that is equal to the minimum annual specialty-specific hour requirement,

(d) has no other certification deficiencies with regard to the substantial involvement or peer review requirements, and

(e) agrees to a written plan to cure the deficiency within the time determined by the committee.

Incomplete Applications

Applications may be denied prior to committee review if candidates fail to provide all requested information and/or pay all applicable fees. These applications are considered incomplete and, as such, are not eligible for committee review.

Denied Applications

Specialty committees may recommend to the board that an application be denied due to insufficiency in any of the standards. Examples include, but are not limited to:

- Licensure: Applicant has recently moved to the state and has not been licensed long enough in the state to meet the standard.

- Substantial Involvement: Applicant does have practice experience but does not meet the minimum total required per year.
- Continuing Legal Education: Applicant has insufficient CLE overall, has insufficient CLE in the practice area, or fails to meet any annual minimum CLE requirements for the practice area.
- Peer Review: Applicant may fail to receive enough completed peer references for the application to proceed or may be reviewed poorly by peers.

Applicants who are denied may wish to appeal the denial. Governing Rules must address the appeal process. The North Carolina State Bar Rules, for example, specify several actions, including the following.

Incomplete Applications

Applicants must submit all necessary information to complete an application within 21 days of the application deadline. Applicants who do not submit all the required information will be denied the opportunity to take a specialty exam. There is no appeal process for this action.

Denial Based on Failure to Meet One or More Standards

Applicants who are denied based on not meeting a particular standard may petition for reconsideration within 14 days of the date of notice.

Reconsideration

A three-member panel of the board is appointed to consider petitions for reconsideration. The panel chair will schedule the hearing to reconsider the application. Alternatively, an applicant can elect to have the matter decided on the written record. In this instance, the applicant will not be present at the hearing and no witnesses shall appear.

Burden of Proof

The standard specifies that the applicant must make a clear and convincing showing that the application satisfies the standards for certification in the applicable specialty.

Panel Decisions

The decision of the panel is binding upon the board. Applicants who receive a denial at this stage may appeal to the North Carolina State Bar Council.

Approved Applications

Applicants who are approved to complete a specialty certification exam receive an approval email with a link to the exam registration form. Applicants select their exam date and must pay the exam fee prior to completion of the exam modules.

Requests for Accommodation

Under the Americans with Disabilities Act, applicants may request accommodations in completion of the necessary exam components for certification. These typically include additional time to complete exam modules and accommodations for either remote exam administration or in-person exam administration. Programs should consider requiring accommodation requests to be made within a set time frame prior to the exam administration. For example, when applicants have been approved to complete a specialty exam and are given an opportunity to register for a specific exam date, accommodation can also be requested at that time. This allows staff sufficient time to coordinate exam schedules, prepare printed copies, or set up remote proctoring as needed.

Financial Program Management

Most legal specialty certification programs run on a tight budget. The North Carolina specialization program is self-supporting and housed within the North Carolina State Bar. See the following sample fee schedule.

Sample fee structure

Initial Certification	Requirements During Certification Period	Recertification
Application fee: $250 Reduced early certification application fee: $200 Examination fee: $200	Certification is effective for five years. Annual fee to maintain certification: $150 At the end of five years, a board-certified specialist must apply for recertification.	Application fee: $250 Specialists do not pay the annual fee during their recertification year.

Fiscal success depends upon lawyers applying for board certification and continuing their certification by paying an annual fee. Efforts need to be made to maintain a strong retention rate of certified lawyers as well. Using the fee schedule presented, a simple estimation of annual income for a small but established program with about 1,000 certified specialists would include:

Fee Type	Number of Payments	Annual Income ($)
Early Application Fee	20	4,000
Application Fee	85	21,250
Examination Fee	90	18,000
Annual Fee	800	120,000
Recertification Fee	200	50,000
Total		**213,250**

Opportunities for Partnership

State certification programs may wish to partner with national certification agencies, as partnerships can provide benefits for both programs. Sample certification partnership options include the following.

Joint Certification

This allows a lawyer to become board certified through both a state and national organization by passing only one exam. For example, applicants for bankruptcy certification in North Carolina may earn certification through both the North Carolina State Bar and the American Board of Certification (ABC) by passing only the ABC exam. Exams are written and graded by the ABC and administered by the North Carolina State Bar.

Applicants must apply to both programs and meet the requirements of each program independently. Fees must also be paid to both programs. In this example, applicants can apply for certification to both agencies at the same time or through either entity first. If a lawyer chooses to apply directly through the ABC, program rules allow applicants to apply for certification with the North Carolina State Bar within two years of passing the ABC bankruptcy exams. The benefit to the lawyer applicant is earning dual certification without completing additional exam modules. The benefits to both the North Carolina State Bar and the ABC are cross-marketing and sharing of resources.

Building Additional Certifications

In this arrangement, lawyers must be certified by one organization (generally a national certifying organization) before applying for certification from another organization. For example, in order to be certified as a specialist in Privacy and Information Security Law from the North Carolina State Bar, an applicant must first have earned the Certified Information Privacy Profession—US Private Sector (CIPP/US) certification through the International Association of Privacy Professionals (IAPP). This allows the North Carolina State Bar Privacy Law Committee members to write, grade, and administer only two exam modules.

Applicants for certification must complete the IAPP CIPP/US exam in the calendar year before, during, or after applying for North Carolina certification. (Example: A lawyer applying for North Carolina State Bar certification in 2025 can pass the CIPP/US exam in 2024, 2025, or 2026.) Certification will be granted upon completion of all certification requirements. The benefit to the lawyer applicant is also earning dual certification without completing additional exam modules. The benefit to the IAPP is that potential applicants for North Carolina State Bar certification must also complete IAPP exam modules. The benefit to the North Carolina State Bar is to limit the workload of committee members.

Scholarships for Public Interest Lawyers

To provide support and encouragement to public interest lawyers, the North Carolina program set up a scholarship fund as a joint initiative with the North Carolina Legal Education Assistance Foundation (NC LEAF). NC LEAF helps North Carolina lawyers pursue careers in public service through educational loan repayment assistance for law school debt. The scholarship fund was launched in 2014 to provide scholarships to pay the application fees for prosecutors, public defenders, and nonprofit public interest lawyers who wish to become certified specialists.

Application fees can be a barrier to applying for certification for attorneys who work in the public sector. This collaboration with NC LEAF furthers the mission of both NC LEAF and the specialization program. Assisting public interest lawyers to seek board certification recognizes commitment to service and encourages these lawyers to continue to serve underrepresented citizens and the public and to improve their knowledge and skills in their practice areas. 100 percent of donations are used to fund scholarships. Scholarship funding is limited, and applicants are encouraged to apply early.

Participating lawyers have accepted positions in which they aid the traditionally underserved populations of North Carolina. They do so at salaries that are often a fraction of those of their counterparts who work at private law firms. Yet they face the same educational debt as their colleagues who enter private practice. A key component of NC LEAF is keeping well-trained attorneys in their jobs, which in turn helps the delivery of justice in the court system and ensures justice for the underrepresented citizens of our state.

In recognition of her long service to the specialization program, the fund was named The Jeri L. Whitfield Legal Specialty Certification Scholarship Fund. Jeri was a board-certified specialist in workers' compensation law from 2000 to 2020 and served as the board chair from 2006 to 2012.

Never-Ending Cycle of Improvement

Exam creation and administration should be thought of as a cycle. Exams should be regularly updated, and results should be reviewed after each administration so that improvements can be made. The following example highlights components that should be addressed annually and those that should be addressed every few years.

Suggested Best Practices

Follow the guidelines given next as part of an ongoing commitment to create and administer specialty exams that are valid, reliable, fair, and consistent.

Exam Blueprints

- Organize all exam questions using category assignments for subject matter
- Review exam assessment details to ensure alignment with exam blueprints
- Review statistical analysis of items to evaluate quality and identify areas for improvement

The exam blueprint is a guide for both the committee members/SMEs and applicants preparing to complete exams. An exam blueprint should have a foundation in job analysis data.

Sample Exam Blueprint Section

Juvenile Delinquency Law	Percentage of Exam Content (based on ranked importance & frequency)	Types of Exam Questions
Secure Custody Shackling 7B-1903 bases for custody Pending disposition & pending placement Constitutional issues Credit for time served	15%	6 multiple-choice 2 short answer
Transfer List of factors Psych evaluation Preparation Evidence Standards Bond issues	15%	2 multiple-choice 1 essay

See Chapter 3 for additional information.

The exam blueprint identifies broad categories of specialty-specific content. This aligns the percentage of the exam that will cover each subject category. Percentages should reflect the relative importance and frequency with which this skill/activity is utilized by a lawyer in the practice area. Continuous improvement includes refining and compiling lists of key and essential skills and classification of objectives (e.g., the cognitive level of skill that you want to measure: knowledge of the law, comprehension of the legal concepts, etc.).

Committee or SME Training

- Provide training opportunities for writing good exam questions and scoring best practices
- Provide exam drafting and grading guidelines to committee members and SMEs

Lawyers, while being quite knowledgeable about their fields of practice, are generally inexperienced at writing valid and reliable exam questions. Program leaders should provide regular training opportunities for these lawyers to learn how to draft questions that provide reliable information about the applicant's competency in the subject matter. Local universities may be a good source for finding trainers who are knowledgeable about item writing and other psychometric concepts.

Exam Grading

- Provide statistical analysis of multiple-choice items for review in scoring the test
- Use objective scoring rubrics for constructed response questions
- Ensure that exams are scored by at least two committee members

Exam grading should be attended by at least three committee members or SMEs. Each grading sheet should be correctly identified by exam number only to ensure confidentiality.

All answers on each exam must be graded. Psychometric analyses of multiple-choice test items should be discussed by the examination committee. Questions with point biserial scores of less than 0.2 (see Chapter 3) should be flagged for discussion and potentially excluded from scoring.

Graders should score the same portions of each exam, noting points and providing optional comments if desired. Graders should review an adequate sample of actual essay answers before grading to develop some sense of likely responses and should adjust grading guides as appropriate. Special care should be taken to ensure that each question is scored by more than one grader and that the final determination is documented for the score on each exam question. In the event of a failure and scheduled exam review, examinees should be given their exam, their answers, and the scoring. Program leaders should decide if any model answers will be provided.

Job Analysis (or Practice Analysis) Process

- Conduct surveys with specialists on regular schedule (every three to five years)
- Collect and use data regarding importance and frequency of job tasks/topics
- Use data to guide exam content and emphasis

The job analysis process is designed to ensure that the exam content aligns with current practice in the subject area. A job analysis survey can systematically examine the tasks, responsibilities, and skills needed to competently perform as a lawyer. Job analysis surveys can be completed using a variety of online survey tools, including Survey Monkey or Google Forms. Surveys should be completed by committee members and a wide variety of specialists to ensure a representative sample. This process includes the following steps:

1. Identify skills and tasks that are necessary for the specific type of legal practice. (Examples for family law include Annulment, Equitable Distribution, Grandparent Visitation, and Termination of Parental Rights.)
2. Create a survey or questionnaire that asks respondents to rate each skill and task as to both frequency and importance.
3. One option is to use a scale of 1–5 (with one being the least frequent or important and five being the most frequent or important).

   Each skill or task will receive an average rating on both frequency and importance. See the following example:

Family Law Skill/Task	Importance	Frequency	Average
Equitable Distribution	4.3	4.6	4.45
Termination of Parental Rights	4.3	2.2	3.25
Grandparent Visitation	3.2	1.8	2.5
Annulment	2.9	2.0	2.45

4. When all survey data has been gathered, each skill or task will have an average rating for both frequency and importance.
5. Provide this information to committee members and SMEs to guide changes in exam content.
6. Committee members will need to review all three columns in the preceding table and make decisions that align the exams with the survey results. In the example provided, equitable distribution would likely take up a larger percentage of the exam than any of the other topics, as it was rated both highly important and very frequently encountered.

Drafting Exam Questions

- Exams can include a mix of multiple-choice questions, short answer questions, and both long and short essay questions.
- Committee members and SMEs should determine the level of knowledge they are seeking with each exam question.
- Bloom's Taxonomy provides a hierarchical model to categorize objectives by level of complexity.

See Chapter 3 for additional information.

Exam Administration Instructions

Care should be taken to ensure that all examinees have the same exam administration instructions and procedures. This limits the possibility of some examinees being unintentionally disadvantaged. Programs should consider adding exam administration instructions and frequently asked questions to their websites as well as emailing instructions to examinees prior to the exam date. Easily accessible instructions help examinees to adequately prepare for what will likely be a stressful exam completion day. As examinees are all professional lawyers, with at least five years of practice experience, they typically have not taken an exam since completing the bar exam. Exam administration instructions vary by state and national organization. One example from North Carolina of exam administration frequently asked questions is available in Appendix A.

Psychometric Analysis

- Perform longitudinal statistical review of multiple-choice exam questions every three years
- Provide details on questions by category or content area
- Flag multiple-choice questions with below 0.2 point biserial scores

See Chapter 3 for additional information.

Cut Score Analysis

- Perform analysis to set cut score during initial exam creation or when significant changes have been made to the exam content or emphasis
- Use bookmark Method, Angoff Method, or other approved method

See Chapter 3 for additional information.

Educational and Study Guide Options

- Use exam blueprint/scoring data to guide articles/study materials and improve the practice of law.

See Chapter 3 for additional information.

Suggested Three-Year Rotation of Best Practices Components

- Complete job analysis surveys
- In-depth psychometric analysis
- Provide educational workshops on writing and grading exam questions

Marketing the Program

When asked, many specialists will indicate that they pursued board certification for lawyers because a colleague encouraged them. Other top reasons for pursuing the program include recognition of enhanced professionalism and a desire to demonstrate a high proficiency level that can be shared within the profession and to potential clients.

Declaration of Intent to Apply

As specialization requires a lengthy preparation to meet the practice and continuing legal education requirements, programs should consider methods of tracking potential applicants. A Declaration of Intent process can help with this tracking. For the North Carolina program, this provides a way for lawyers to connect with staff and begin the application process up to five years in advance. The declaration can be tracked with something as simple as an online form (both Google and Microsoft offer these) that allows the data to be pulled into a spreadsheet for easy review. Lawyers can file a Declaration of Intent to Apply with no fee and no commitment. The form asks for name, email address, state bar number, intended practice area, and planned year of application.

Logos/Badges

Providing logos and badges to specialists allows them to easily identify their accomplishment to potential clients and to the legal community. Encourage consistent use of program-approved verbiage and visual markers among specialists. This begins to build a brand that is recognizable among lawyers. Branding helps build a pool of potential specialists and allows current specialists to participate in marketing the program.

Ensure that specialists understand the value that certification can bring to their practice. Board certification can help lawyers leverage a powerful differentiator when used consistently across all marketing channels, including social media, ads, email signatures, and websites. Survey results have shown that members of the public value board certification, selecting the board-certified option over a lawyer with more years of experience 63 percent of the time (survey findings available at nclawspecialists.gov/infographic/).

Sample Logo

BOARD OF LEGAL SPECIALIZATION
NORTH CAROLINA STATE BAR
Employment Law

Sample Badge

BOARD CERTIFIED

Employment Law

BETA Exam Process

New specialty programs should begin by creating a BETA exam. Completing a BETA exam process allows the program to open the newly created exam to a smaller applicant pool to test the validity and reliability of exam questions before launching the specialty exam to a wider audience. One example of the BETA exam process follows.

Create the Exam Blueprint

A. Gather committee members and SMEs to draw up an exhaustive list of the tasks and skills used in the practice area.

B. Use this list to create the Job (Practice) Analysis Survey.

   1. Each skill and task should be rated in terms of both frequency and importance.
   2. Survey respondents will provide rating information based on their own personal experience as a practitioner.
   3. Survey results will be used to determine the coverage of each skill or task on the exam blueprint. See family law example on page 39.

C. Confirm BETA exam blueprint.

Draft Exam Questions

A. Committee members and SMEs determine what types of questions will be used on the exam: multiple choice, short answer, short and/or long essay.

B. Committee members and SMEs determine how to match skills/tasks with question types. For example, the North Carolina State Bar Employment Law BETA exam structure included the following:

Discrimination in Employment	Approximately 38% of Exam Topics
Age Discrimination in Employment Act of 1967 Americans with Disabilities Protection Act Genetic Information Nondiscrimination Act (GINA) Older Worker Benefits Protection Act Section 1981 of the Civil Rights Act of 1866 Title VII of the Civil Rights Act of 1964	**Discrimination in Employment:** Estimated 9 short answer, 1 essay, and 17 multiple-choice questions

C. Committee members and SMEs will begin to draft exam questions based on the exam blueprint.

D. Each potential exam question submitted must include the model answer.

E. Essay and short answer questions must also include a breakdown of how points will be allocated.

Additional Recommendations

A. Initial committees are made up of 10–12 members or SMEs.

B. Regularly scheduled meetings are set up to review potential questions and model answers.

C. Subcommittees focusing on specific skills/tasks or specific types of questions can help with motivation and achieving targeted numbers of exam questions by specific dates.

D. The entire process should be scheduled over approximately a six-month period if committee members and SMEs are volunteers.
E. Exam questions are organized by type and topic for review and revision at each scheduled meeting.
F. Additional subcommittee meetings may be needed to ensure that questions meet the guidelines.

See Chapter 3 for additional information.

Piloting the BETA Exam

Potential BETA exam takers should be practitioners that meet the requirements to become board-certified specialists. A wide range of experience levels, genders, and types of practices is recommended to ensure that the exam is fair to all who may apply. The North Carolina State Bar BETA exam process involves examinees receiving an exam fee waiver for their participation in the process. BETA exam takers must also participate in a meeting with committee members and SMEs to provide feedback on the exam. This includes difficulty level of exam questions, distribution of content, and clarity of expected answers. Additionally, they may apply for certification prior to the exam administration or following receipt of their pass/fail status. One example of this process follows:

- Recruit potential BETA exam takers.
- Schedule a testing date and location (or remote administration).
- Provide exam registration materials to BETA exam takers.
- Provide application materials for those who choose to apply early.
- Provide exam guide information and any applicable study tips.
- Administer BETA exam.
- Schedule committee members and SMEs to score exams and determine preliminary pass/fail results.

- Complete BETA exam feedback sessions.
- Work with psychometrician to determine cut score, based on preliminary scoring and feedback.

Reporting Exam Results

The first class of certified specialists can include both committee members and BETA exam takers who received a passing score on the exam and chose to apply early (assuming they meet the other requirements for certification). This ensures that the new specialty is off to a good start with a strong first class of specialists. The recommendation here is to deliver only a pass or fail notification. For example, the North Carolina program allows lawyers who fail an exam to review the results, but a lawyer who passes an exam only receives the indication of a passing score. This protects the security and confidentiality of the exam questions and limits unnecessary work for the staff.

Appendix A

Sample Instructions Governing the Specialty Exams from the North Carolina State Bar Website

Exam Location

Q: When and where is the exam taking place?

A: The Exam Calendar is available on the website.

Specialty Certification Exams are offered through ExamSoft Remote Proctoring as well as through in-person exam administration. Please review the Exam Calendar to see which practice areas are scheduled for in-person exams. Accommodation may be granted if conditions allow.

Q: An emergency came up and I am unable to sit for the exam. What should I do?

A: Please notify the state bar as soon as possible. There may be an alternate test date available. If not, in most cases, you can reapply the following year, pay $50 and not have to resubmit peer references.

Q: What time should I be prepared to start my exam?

A: **Be prepared early.** Please be ready before 8:00 am for check-in and locating the exam passwords. The exam modules will begin promptly at 8:15 am.

Exam Day

Q: Where can I find out what days my examination is being held?

A: Dates can be found on the Exam Calendar on the website.

Q: I would like to take my exam on the computer. What do I need to do?

A: Most exams are offered only by computer. You will need to provide your own laptop and you will need to download the exam software two weeks prior to exam day. Additional information about the computerized exam software is available on the website. *Bankruptcy exams are offered by handwriting or through typing essay answers on a laptop through a word processing program.

Q: I would prefer to handwrite my exam. What do I need to do?

A: Specialty certification exams will not have a handwriting option, except for bankruptcy law.

Q: Will the exam have my name or other personal information on it?

A: No, all exam registrants will be assigned an exam number. This examination number will be used on all exams in the exam software. The examinee should not type any identifying information in the software. The exams are graded and referred to by their examination number to maintain anonymity.

Q: Can I use my own books, papers, or personal effects during the examination?

A: Books and Papers: Only appellate practice, bankruptcy, criminal, juvenile delinquency, and utilities examinees are allowed to bring open book materials. See the Exam Guides for further information. Before the exams begin, examinees will need to put away all books, papers, and personal effects.

Calculators: Some practice areas allow specialty examinees to bring a calculator, but any such calculator must be silent. You may not use the calculator on your cell phone. To prevent disruption in the examination area (for in-person exams), please do not use watches that emit a periodic beep. All cell phones must be turned off. The software will inform you of the time remaining in each examination session.

Other materials: Only materials approved by the staff may be used during the examination.

Personal effects: Disposable ear plugs are permitted; ear buds and headphones are NOT permitted. Items like ChapStick and cough drops are permitted as well as personal water bottles and/or coffee mugs. For any items not mentioned, please contact staff to inquire.

Q: Can I use a calculator?

A: Only bankruptcy, estate planning, social security, and workers' compensation law specialty examinees may bring a calculator. Any such calculator must be silent. The calculator will be activated on the software for those specialty areas as well. You may not use the calculator on your cell phone.

Q: How long is the exam?

A: Most exams are a total of 6 hours. The morning of exam day will include two 90-minute exam modules followed by an hour break for lunch. The afternoon of exam day will begin by 1:30 pm and will also include two 90-minute exam modules ending at approximately 4:45 pm. You may not need the entire 90 minutes to complete any of the exam modules. The exceptions to these times are appellate practice, bankruptcy, privacy, and real property law exams. Please see the following questions for more information.

Q: Can I finish any of the exam sessions early?

A: Yes, you may submit your exam modules when you have finished.

Q: I am taking the appellate, bankruptcy, privacy, or real property law exam. How is my exam structured?

A: Examinees taking the **appellate practice exam**:

Exam Day 1: Traditional exam modules in the morning include multiple choice and short essay questions. Examinees will receive a packet containing the take-home exam portion. The take-home exam is due approximately 10 days later. Instructions regarding the exam will be included in the take home exam packet.

Examinees taking the **bankruptcy law exam**:[1]

Exam Day 1: General exam in the morning and subspecialty (business or consumer) in the afternoon.

Exam Day 2: Three-hour exam for examinees taking second subspecialty (business or consumer).

Examinees taking the **privacy and information security exam**:

Exam Day 1: Three-hour exam for examinees which may be scheduled in the morning (8:15 start time) or in the afternoon (1:00 start time). Please contact staff if you have questions.

Examinees taking the **real property law exam:**[2]

Exam Day 1: General and title portion of exam in the morning and subspecialty (commercial or residential) in the afternoon.

Exam Day 2: Three-hour exam for examinees taking second subspecialty (commercial or residential)

Restroom Breaks

Q: Are we allowed to get up to use the restroom during the exam?

A: No, you must complete the exam module before you leave the room or take a break. The 90-minute exam modules allow for short breaks between sessions. Please use the restroom during the breaks and do not leave the room until you have submitted your exam module.

---

1. The order in which the exam is administered may vary depending on exam location and date. Please contact staff if you have questions.

2. The order in which the exam is administered may vary depending on exam location and date. Please contact staff if you have questions.

Lunch/Refreshments

Q: Is there a lunch break between the morning and afternoon exam sessions?

A: Yes. The lunch break will begin at approximately 12 pm. Examinees need to return to their exam location to begin checking in for the afternoon session at 1 pm. For on-site exams, applicants may prefer to bring lunch or have it delivered.

Exam Guides/Subject Matter Outlines

Q: Where can I find information on what will be on the exam?

A: You can review the exam guide or subject matter outline for your specialty.

Q: What other resources might help me with studying for the exam?

A: You may find it helpful to talk with a mentor in your specialty area. We provide an exam mentor list of specialists that have recently taken the exam and have volunteered to be a point of contact for any questions you may have.

Exam Content

Q: What if I have a question about the exam content during the examination session?

A: If you have a question regarding format or typos, please let the staff know following the exam session by emailing staff.

Q: Should I include recent developments when answering exam questions?

A: Answers to the examination questions should be given in terms of substantive law as it exists on the day of the examination. All recent developments are fair game. Assume that the exam contains a logical question and answer under that assumption.

Exam Open Book Materials

Q: Will my exam have open book materials?

A: Only appellate practice, bankruptcy, criminal, juvenile delinquency, social security disability, utilities, and workers' compensation law exams require or provide open book materials. If you have any questions about what open materials are allowed or provided, refer to the exam guides on the legal specialization website. If you are still unsure, please contact staff.

Exam Grading

Q: Who grades the exams?

A: The exams are graded by the corresponding specialty committees with the exception of the bankruptcy and elder law exams, which are graded by the individual organizations that sponsor the exams.

Q: How are exams with subspecialties graded?

A: Examinees seeking certification in both bankruptcy and real property subspecialties will be graded separately on each examination of the two subspecialties. An examinee will be certified as a specialist in only one of the two subspecialties if the examinee passes only one of the examinations.

Exam Results

Q: When will exam results be available?

A: For the specialty areas of appellate practice, child welfare law, criminal law, estate planning, family law, juvenile delinquency, immigration law, social security disability law, privacy and information security law, real property law, trademark law, utilities law, and workers' compensation law, you may check your exam results at 2 pm on December 8 on the State Bar specialization website. For the elder law and bankruptcy specialties, exam results are available three-four months after this date. For more information visit nelf.org or www.abcworld.org.

Q: I sat for an exam with two subspecialties and didn't pass one. What happens now?

A: Examinees seeking certification in both bankruptcy and real property law subspecialties will be graded separately on each examination of the two subspecialties. An examinee will be certified as a specialist in only one of the two subspecialties if the examinee passes only one of the examinations. Once you take and pass one subspecialty, you can re-take the other subspecialty at any time without having to take the general portion of the exam again.

Chapter 3

Creating, Administering, Scoring, and Maintaining a Legal Specialty Examination

Terry Ackerman

Assembling, administering, scoring, and maintaining a legal specialty exam can be a major endeavor. Specialty examinations are closely related to professional certification and licensure examinations (e.g., certifying medical specializations or expertise or licensing accountants). Credentialing organizations are usually nongovernmental agencies that emerge from professional societies or professional interest groups. Most certifications result in titles or low-to-moderate-stakes credentials issued as part of a voluntary credentialing process. In contrast, licensure is usually a regulatory process resulting from legislation or an executive order to protect the public against potential harm or injury from unsafe or otherwise inappropriate professional practices. Despite some differences from specialty examinations, most of the steps outlined in this chapter draw from the literature on those types of examinations (see, for example, Raymond & Luecht, 2013; Luecht, 2017).

This chapter outlines a nine-step process. Each step details the procedures involved and provides specific examples from legal specialty exams used in North Carolina—specifically drawing on documentation developed by the specialty exam committees and comprising the North Carolina State Bar Board of Legal

Specialization Exam Manual (Mullen, 2024). The logistics of several of the measurement processes discussed briefly in this chapter are presented in more logistical detail in Chapter 2 (e.g., job analysis, exam administration, reporting test results).

Before moving into the nine steps, two strong recommendations are offered. First, include a measurement expert on any specialty committee or some other authorized group that sets policies and oversees the creation, administration, scoring, and scale maintenance for the specialty examination. Including a measurement expert on that type of committee or group can help avoid technical issues and even legal challenges to the accuracy and validity of the scores and decisions made. That is, a measurement expert can help explain the measurement theory behind writing items, setting up rubrics, establishing one or more cut scores, and interpreting test results. Most measurement experts are also well aware of the *Standards for Educational and Psychological Testing* (APA, AERA & NCME, 2014) that help ensure the quality and fairness of tests.

The second recommendation is to document everything at a detailed level. The goal is to have a living history of the development of the specialty exam, scoring decisions, standard-setting procedures, and job analyses. This documentation will enable the specialty examination committee to defend challenges to the test results, educate new committee members, and have guidelines for future test improvement. The idea that a specialty exam committee should continuously seek improvement aligns with the pursuit of excellence. By maintaining a commitment to refining their assessments, committee members can enhance the quality and accuracy of their evaluations. This approach ensures that the tests remain relevant and effective for evaluating candidates' knowledge and skills.

Step 1: Specify the Purpose and Inferences

At the outset, an examination committee is usually selected from lawyers the bar recognizes as "experts" in that specialty. This committee is generally composed of five or six members. To start with, the committee members must define the purpose of the specialty test and the specific inferences they want to draw from the results. Committee members need to discuss what it means to be further certified as a specialist. What are the expectations and intended inferences that can be drawn from one's test performance, both for those who meet and exceed the set standard and for those who do not? Here is a specific example from the N.C. Bar Specialty Exam Manual:

> The purpose of certification is two-fold:
>
> (1) to assist in the delivery of legal services to the public by identifying to the public those lawyers who have demonstrated special knowledge, skill, and proficiency in a specific field, so that the public can more closely match its needs with available services; and
>
> (2) to improve the competency of the bar by establishing an additional incentive for lawyers to participate in continuing legal education and meet the other requirements of specialization.

The committee must also identify which lawyers are eligible to take the specialty exam. What are the requirements necessary to be eligible to take the examination? (Note: In North Carolina, to be eligible a lawyer must have practiced in the specialty for at least five years and have three letters of recommendation that support their standing in the specialty.)

Step 2: Create a Test Content Framework

The committee needs to develop a test content framework that describes the breadth and depth of the knowledge and skills to be assessed. This framework ultimately leads to the design of a test content blueprint that specifies item counts in various content areas, item types, and so on. Committee members are usually subject matter experts (SMEs). They need to articulate the relevant competencies and prioritize the key knowledge and skills needed to support competency-based claims. That is, the SMEs need to detail what body of knowledge needs to be assessed and the types of items that can best assess each competency. In other words, substantively what legal knowledge should specialists be required to know and at what level of cognition should this be assessed?

Most test content frameworks for credentialing examinations are developed as the outcome of a survey research study known as "practice analysis." A practice analysis might sample and survey entry-level professionals in a discipline or front-line supervisors familiar with the required knowledge and skills of new hires. Educators can also be surveyed to provide their perspectives. A practice analysis focuses on the duration and criticality of tasks actually performed in professional practice (Raymond, 2001; Raymond & Neustel, 2006; Raymond & Luecht, 2013). That is, the practice analysis helps to identify both the most prevalent and the most critical tasks performed by the intended population of examinees. The priorities that emerge from the practice analysis form part of the evidentiary validity argument as to what the examination measures and can be directly reflected in a test content blueprint—described later.

The results from a practice analysis can be supplemented by also considering the requisite cognitive complexity intended for the test items. For example, Bloom's rather famous taxonomy has six levels of cognitive knowledge and skills (Bloom et al., 1956; see Figure 3.1): Knowledge, Comprehension, Application,

Analysis, Synthesis, and Evaluation. The later five categories identify "skills and abilities" that require "knowledge" as a precondition. These categories and accompanying verbal descriptors can help the exam committee members convert the prioritized task statements obtained from practice analyses into more targeted item-writing specifications reflecting specific levels of cognition. For example, one could ask questions just at the knowledge level, in which case primarily memorization of facts is required. However, one could test at the evaluation level, in which case a question would ask the examinee to review a fact pattern and then compare and contrast arguments extracted from the fact pattern. The examination should be as realistic as possible and mirror the day-to-day responsibilities and required activities of the specialty.

Although Bloom's taxonomy is now considered to be "outdated" by most cognitive scientists, it still provides a logical way to guide the development of the content framework. A more recent taxonomy used extensively in educational testing is the four-level "depth of knowledge" (Webb, 1997).

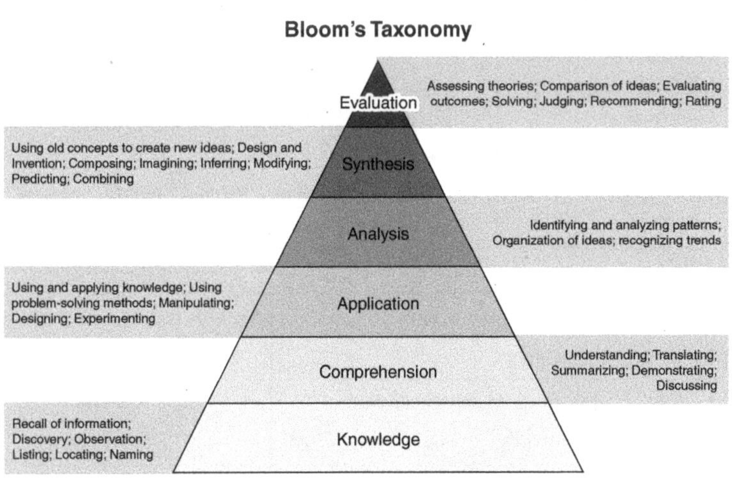

FIGURE 3.1 A pyramid diagram illustrating the six levels of cognition in Bloom's taxonomy and defining tasks that exemplify each level.

Step 3: Build Test Specifications

The committee needs to translate the content framework into detailed test specifications called a "test blueprint." The blueprint outlines the item-count allocations relative to key content areas, item formats, and potentially the cognitive level of the assessment. They should also include the number and types of items, time limits, and scoring rules. Each committee member could be assigned to one part of the exam so that the work involved in the test development is shared equally. The specifications allow the committee to step back from the process and ensure that everything required for the specialist to be further certified has been identified.

Here is an example of test specifications for the Juvenile Delinquency Specialty Examination in North Carolina.

Specialty Area and Contact	Exam Date	Question Summary
Juvenile Delinquency— Subspecialty of criminal law (contact: Chair of the Specialty Committee)	10/22 BETA or 10/28	Module 1: Gen Crim (125 points) Module 2: (125 points) Module 3: (125 points) Module 4: (125 points) 50 multiple-choice questions: 2.5 points 2 short essays: 25 points 20 short answer: 10 points

Part II Juvenile Delinquency Law	% imp.	
Intake and Interview	4%	
• Role of lawyer/duty of express interest • Timeliness (*In re* DS) • Nondivertibles • 7B-2408 issue • Postdiversion approval/deferred prosecution		2 multiple choice 2 short answer

Part II Juvenile Delinquency Law	**% imp.**	
Secure Custody	15%	
• Shackling (3rd SCR = rehear?) • 7B-1903 bases for custody • "pending dispo" & "pending placement" • constitutional issues • credit for time served		6 multiple choice 2 short answer
Probable Cause	5%	
• Waive or not • *In re* JJ Jr. • Constitutional issues with 1* murder • Recusal PC to transfer PC to adjudication • Juv proffer of evidence • State's evidence (just enough or mini-trial?)		1 short answer
Transfer	15%	
• List of factors • Psych evaluation • Preparation • Evidence Standards? • Bond issues		2 multiple choice 1 essay
Motions to Suppress	15%	
• JDB v. NC *In re* KDL (vs. *In re* WR) • Search/seizure issues *In re* TAS *In re* DB (2011 N.C. App. Lexis 1745) *In re* KTL (nonschool drug search—reasonable juv) • Mechanics of hearing/voir dire • Preserving issues		One long essay

Part II Juvenile Delinquency Law	**% imp.**	
Adjudicatory Hearings	7%	
• 7B-2405 (judge protecting kids' rights) • *In re* JRV (court must advise of right against self-incrimination prior to kid testifying) • Petition sufficiency • Petition amendment • Timing of motions to VD • When does jeopardy attach? • Evidence • Strategy question for State & defense • Closed vs. open courtroom (7B-2402)		3 multiple choice 3 short answer 1 essay
Disposition Hearings	15%	
• List of available dispo conditions (MC) • Points—figuring out levels • Collateral consequences Felony policy of HSAA Immigration issues Education Military Vocational Impact on later cases (point system) • Restitution Joint & several Ability to pay Court's findings of fact • *In re* DAQ		11 multiple choice 1 short answer 1 long essay
Probation/Motions for Review	10%	
• List of options • Exposure (what can court do?) • Hearing & evidence Standard		5 multiple choice 1 short answer
Commitment to Youth Development Centers	7%	
• *In re* JSW • Credit time served • Legal basis • Arguments for and against commitment • Community commitment		1 short answer

Part II Juvenile Delinquency Law	**% imp.**	
Appeals and Postdisposition Issues	7%	
• Both motions to VD (preservation) Timing • Sufficiency of evidence • Release pending appeal • 2600 motions		1 multiple choice 1 essay

The committee must decide the best way or type of item needed to assess each content element.

Item types could include multiple choice, short answer, or essay. Note that true-false items are not recommended for specialty exams. In every situation, the items should accurately depict the challenges that a lawyer encounters in their day-to-day activities within their specific field of expertise.

The percentages or weights assigned to each content area reflect the committee's perspective of the importance of that area. There is no one-size-fits-all when it comes to test specifications. For the same specialization area, these could vary from state to state.

These blueprints need to be reviewed every year by the committee to make the test reflect current practice. As previously noted, a practice analysis can update the skills and knowledge required to be assessed (e.g., every three to five years). In this context, the practice analysis would involve surveying a representative sample of lawyers in the specialty about the current skills being assessed and if there are any new skills or competencies that need to be added.

To ensure that the 14 specialty exams are uniform in their content and format, the North Carolina Bar has established the policy that each exam must meet the following requirements:

Total Exam Points: 500 – Passing Score: 350 (unless otherwise set through the cut-score procedure)

Question/Time Guidelines

- 35 multiple choice questions per 1 hour period – maximum
- 1 long essay question per 1 hour period – maximum
- 4 short essay questions per 1 hour period – maximum
- 10 short answer questions per 1 hour period – maximum

If questions involve long fact patterns or other substantial case information, the committee must allow for a reasonable amount of reading time. The reading time will lessen the amount of questions allowed in the guidelines as listed above.

Several formats for the total test are suggested, including:

<u>Morning Session 1</u>: 1 long essay question worth 25 points and 10 short answer questions worth 10 points each = 125 points
<u>Morning Session 2</u>: 1 long essay question worth 25 points and 10 short answer questions worth 10 points each = 125 points
<u>Afternoon Session 1</u>: 50 multiple choice questions worth 2.5 points each = 125 points
<u>Afternoon Session 2</u>: 50 multiple choice questions worth 2.5 points each = 125 points

or

<u>Morning Session 1</u>: 5 short essay questions worth 20 points each = 100 points
<u>Morning Session 2</u>: 5 short essay questions worth 20 points each = 100 points

Afternoon Session 1: 30 multiple choice questions worth five points each = 150 points
Afternoon Session 2: 15 short answer questions worth 10 points each = 150 points

Step 4: Generate Potential Test Items and Develop Scoring Rubrics

The next step is for committee members to generate the test items using the test specifications.

This is probably the most challenging step in the process. This task is usually divided among the committee members depending on the subareas of expertise. It is wise to generate more items than required. All items that are created should be placed into an examination item bank. Remember, writing items is not part of anyone's genetic code or DNA; you just get better at doing it through practice. There are some excellent sources on writing high-quality test items (e.g., Case & Swanson, 2003; Haladyna, 2004; Haladyna & Rodriguez, 2013).

Next are general guidelines that should be followed in developing the different item types.

Multiple-Choice Items

First, it is necessary to understand the terminology used by test developers.

The factual situation itself is called the **stimulus**. The portion of the stimulus that sets forth the question is called the **stem**. The possible answers are referred to as **options**, and the correct answer is called the **key**. Incorrect options are referred to as **distractors**.

General guidelines for writing multiple-choice items include the following:

- Topics covered should follow exactly from the test specifications and not deal with "fringe" or obscure issues.
- The stimulus should be brief but present all necessary information to answer the item.
- The stem should present a clear, unambiguous question. The competent examinee should not struggle to determine what is being asked. Double negatives should be avoided.
- Options should be similar in terms of focus and length.
- Four options should be sufficient, as creating plausible distractors becomes more difficult with more than four options.
- Absolute terms such as "always" or "never" should not be used.
- The key must be the correct answer to the stem's question.
- Options such as "all of the above" or "none of the above" encourage guessing and stand out from the other options and therefore should be avoided.
- Distractors should not be drafted to "trick" examinees but should evaluate competency levels, not just test-taking skills.

Multiple-choice items can have three formats: **Common**, **Item Set (Grouping)**, and **Combined**.

The **Common** format is the most familiar and consists of three parts:

- Part 1 (the stimulus) contains a fact pattern with all the facts necessary to resolve the problem.
- Part 2 (the stem) is a question to be answered or an introduction to the choices.
- Part 3 (options) lists options containing both distractors and the key.

In this format, distractors need to have diagnostic value. That is, each distractor should provide insight into the incorrect reasoning of the examinee. For example:

(A) Yes, because
(B) No, because
(C) Yes, because
(D) No, because

Here is an example of a Common multiple-choice item from the N.C. Juvenile Delinquency Exam:

> Assuming that a jurisdiction has a restitution program that paid $3.00 per hour for community service work and a juvenile has been ordered to do community service in order to pay restitution, what is the maximum amount that the juvenile can be ordered to pay through community service for a level 1 disposition?
>
> A. $355
>
> B. $300*
>
> C. $710
>
> D. $500
>
> E. $120

In the **Item Set** (Grouping) format, there is one fact pattern, followed by a series of separate multiple-choice questions. The stimulus describes a hypothetical scenario and then is followed by two or three multiple-choice questions that are all based on the presented fact pattern.

The **Combined** format contains a two-level option design. These are considered more difficult than the other multiple-choice questions and generally take longer to answer. There are three parts:

- Part 1 (the stimulus): The fact pattern, which contains all of the necessary facts.
- Part 2 (the stem): The question to be answered followed by statements of the law or propositions to be considered; for example:

Which of the following statements reflects A's rights?

I. A may declare an immediate breach . . . .
II. A may demand further assurances . . . .
III. A may cover by purchasing a . . . .

- Part 3 (the options) reflects different statement combinations.
  (A) I only
  (B) I and II only
  (C) I, II, and III
  (D) I and III only

An example of a Combined multiple-choice question from the Juvenile Delinquency Specialty Exam follows:

Appeals can be made from:

1. Any order of adjudication
2. Any order finding absence of jurisdiction
3. Any order of disposition after adjudication
4. Any order modifying custodial rights
5. Any order contrary to the best interests of the juvenile

A. 1, 2, and 3
B. 1, 3, and 4
C. 2, 3, and 4*
D. 1, 3, 4, and 5
E. 3, 4, and 5

Short Answer and Essay Questions

Short answer and essay items require examinees to write a detailed response to a question or prompt. The difference between the two is only in the length of the expected response: essay items tend to be longer, requiring several paragraphs. Unlike a multiple-choice item, responding to a short answer or essay item requires the examinee to generate a response versus selecting a correct answer. A big advantage of these items is that they allow examinees to demonstrate their understanding, critical thinking, and ability to synthesize information. These items also assess the ability to organize thoughts, articulate ideas, and construct coherent arguments. The drawback is that essay and short answer items require longer response time. Scoring these items can be subjective unless a well-developed rubric guides the scoring process. Essay questions cannot cover as many topics as multiple-choice items can.

Essay questions can be designed to assess the following abilities:

- Identify legal issues raised by a hypothetical fact situation.
- Express an understanding of the fundamental legal principles relevant to the probable solution of the issues raised by the fact situation.
- Apply the law to the facts or situations to resolve.
- Present a reasoned analysis of the relevant issues in a clear, concise, and well-organized composition.
- Separate material that is relevant from that which is not.
- Communicate in writing effectively.
- Use higher-order thinking skills such as synthesis and evaluation. Bloom's taxonomy chart provides item writers with the appropriate descriptors or verbiage to elicit different levels of cognitive ability.

Bloom's Taxonomy Chart	
Knowledge (Recalling learned material)	recall, underline, list, name, record, label, cluster, match, memorize, define, arrange
Comprehension (Understanding the material)	understand, show, summarize, explain, describe, demonstrate, review, cite, restate, locate
Application (Using the material)	apply, select, model, organize, illustrate, utilize, choose, imitate, demonstrate, use
Analysis (Breaking material down to increase understanding)	analyze, compare, contrast, classify, map, characterize, divide, break down, choose, examine
Synthesis (Reshaping material into a new form)	construct, speculate, design, compose, create, develop, invent, blend, propose, formulate
Evaluation (Judging the worth of material)	evaluate, convince, argue, judge, criticize, rate, measure, persuade, assess, recommend

Table 3.1 A chart listing verbal descriptors that elicit responses that require different levels of cognition as identified in Bloom's taxonomy.

Other guidelines for creating short answer and essay questions include the following:

1. Questions should be based on legal principles and theories of general application and should not require obscure, technical, or little-known statutory or common law provisions. Each question should contain two or more issues (depending on the time allowed for applicants to answer the question), and it should be presented in such a manner as to call for an independent discussion of each issue. If there is a possibility of concluding either way on one issue, discussing the other issues should not depend upon which conclusion is reached on the first.

2. These questions should be drafted so that the examinees can perceive what points of law are involved and what discussion is expected. The hypothetical fact scenario should be lucid and grammatically correct. Plain language, short sentences, and frequent paragraphs should be used.
3. Sometimes these questions may contain intended factual ambiguities designed to test whether the examinee comprehends the need to obtain more facts to resolve the question adequately and sees that unrevealed information may change assumptions and outcomes. However, questions should not contain unintentional ambiguities or irrelevancies.
4. One problem with this item type is that it is difficult to develop a uniform set of grading criteria if some candidates ignore irrelevant facts and concentrate in depth on the crucial issues while some identify and dispose of every fact, including irrelevant ones, but handle all superficially. Graders cannot differentiate between those who do not discuss an irrelevant fact because they did not see it and those who did not discuss it because they have dismissed it as irrelevant. Graders should never assume the examinee meant or knows something that is not articulated in writing.
5. Never use names that are whimsical or pejorative or that have racial, political, or sociological overtones. Such names tend to distract the applicants and detract from the validity of the question. Use functional names that refer to the role the character assumes (e.g., *Victim*, *Pilot*, *Author*, *Doctor*, *Nurse*, *Broker*, *Seller*, *Buyer*, *Pedestrian*, *Husband*). Names can also begin with letters that follow an alphabetical sequence or make logical sense in the law. For example, names that start with P and D may be used to designate plaintiff and defendant. Gender-neutral names should be used whenever possible. Avoid using two or more names that begin with the same letter.

6. Pay careful attention to the question framed at the end of the facts. The specific task assigned to the candidate must be unmistakably clear, and it must be clear that a discussion, as opposed to a mere conclusion, is required. Examples of questions include: "How should the court rule on each item in Buyer's motion? Explain." "To whom should Testator's estate be distributed?" Avoid the pitfall of phrasing a question that can be answered with a one-word response: "Is Seller liable?"
7. Be mindful of the total amount of time allocated to the question (e.g., 30 minutes); the applicant will need sufficient time to read and outline the question and then write the answer. Exam directions should identify the length of the answer that is expected as well as the length of time allowed to generate the answer.
8. It is important to create an expected response including relevant authorities for both short answer and essay items. This response can then be used to create a scoring rubric that details how points are to be awarded. Scoring rubrics indicate the relative importance of the issues and the level of performance an examinee must achieve for each possible score level. Rubrics must be clear and defensible.

Following is an example of a short 20-point question and corresponding scoring rubric for the Bankruptcy Specialty Exam:

> Question 3. In February 2014, Atlantic Microwave, an insolvent North Carolina corporation, suspended its business operations. Shortly thereafter, on February 25, 2014, an undersecured creditor with a lien on inventory observed movement of assets out of the business premises. A secured creditor also received information that the corporation had repaid several loans to its officers during the preceding 120 days. The creditor consults counsel who recommends that a North Carolina receivership might be the appropriate remedy. (20 points)

a. What type of judge can appoint a receiver for Atlantic Microwave?

b. Under the circumstances, would the court appoint a receiver?

c. Can a receiver recover the payments made to its officers?

Q. 3	Point Value – 20	Answer	Points Awarded
a.	5	Superior Court Judge	
b.	5	Yes, a receiver can be appointed where loss of property may occur.	
c.	10	Yes, the Uniform Fraudulent Transfer Act, section 39-23.5, provides that a transfer made by a debtor is voidable as to a creditor whose claim arose before the transfer was made if the transfer was made to an insider for an antecedent debt, the debtor was insolvent at the time, and the insider had reasonable cause to believe that the debtor was insolvent.	
Total			

Here is an example of an Estate Planning essay question:

ESTATE PLANNING DOCUMENTS AND PROCEDURES: Mudd Family: Ronald Mudd, age 60, is married to Jane Mudd, age 55, and they have three children: Raoul Mudd, age 35, is a practicing surgeon, is married, and has two children, ages 12 and 6; Stephanie M. Mudd, age 32, is married – her husband is a computer programmer – and has one child, age 8; and Melanie Mudd, age 30, is unmarried, but has a child, age 4. The

Communist Workers Party employs her and she corresponds infrequently with her parents, visiting them only on rare occasions. All of the children and grandchildren are North Carolina residents except for Melanie and her child, who live in California.

Estate Facts: Following his making of an appointment with you to get advice on appropriate estate planning documents, Ronald Mudd has presented to you detailed information with regard to his assets at the present time, which are:

Cash and Money Market Accounts	$1,000,000
Marketable Securities	20,000,000
Life Insurance (Face Amount)	2,000,000
Residence	275,000
Rental Real Estate	300,000
Personal Property and Personal Effects	10,000
Current Gross Estate	$13,585,000

The income currently being produced by his assets amounts to $835,000 as follows:

Cash and Money Market Accounts	$5,000
Marketable Securities	800,000
Rental Real Estate	30,000
Total Income from Assets	$835,000

At your initial conference, Ronald Mudd indicated that the primary intentions with regard to disposition of his estate are that his wife be amply provided for during her remaining lifetime and that death taxes be minimized so as to provide a maximum amount to be left to his family. He also indicates to you that, following the death of his wife, he would prefer that funds be provided on a preferential basis to care for his daughters and their children rather than for his son, whose education and medical training have been financed by Ronald and who is commencing to build an independent estate. In addition, he inquires about a procedure whereby only limited funds be made available to his daughter, Melanie, whom he considers unreliable and imprudent.

a) Discuss in the space provided below and on the following page the estate plan (lifetime and at death) that you would recommend for Ronald and his family, including (if appropriate) testamentary and inter vivos trusts.

b) Discuss the dispositive provisions you would recommend for Ronald's will and trusts to carry out his primary testamentary intentions and planning objectives [Do not discuss the selection of fiduciaries (See question (c), below)].

c) Discuss in the space provided below the factors to be considered in the selection of fiduciaries under Ronald's will and any testamentary or inter vivos trusts included in the estate plan recommended in question (a), above. State also your recommendations as to the specific fiduciaries to be selected by Ronald.

The following answers to the previous questions were drafted by the Estate Planning committee.

a) Because of the size of Ronald's estate, an estate plan would be recommended which would take full advantage of the unlimited marital deduction under the federal estate tax law. In addition, it would be appropriate to make use of the federal unified credit shelter share, so that this amount would be excluded from the taxable estate of Ronald's wife, Jane, at her death. Due regard would be reserved to provide an inheritance for the Mudd daughters, Stephanie and Melanie, providing supervision for the investment of Stephanie's trust for a limited period of time and permanent provisions for the administration and preservation of an estate or funds for Melanie, including possibly a provision for Melanie by an inter vivos trust.

Provisions for generation-skipping bequests to the children of Raoul Mudd would be recommended within the amount of the GST exemption.

b) Exemption equivalent bequests (subject to payment of death taxes) to Ronald's daughters, Stephanie and Melanie, in trust with the trust income payable to his wife and/or daughters and his residuary estate to a qualified marital trust for Jane with remainder, or contingent bequests of the residue if Jane predeceases, trusts for his daughters with a $1,000,000 bequest to the children of Raoul in minority trusts; Stephanie's trust would terminate when she attained age 45, the remainder interest passing to Stephanie; Melanie's trust would terminate upon the death of the survivor of Jane or Melanie and would pass to Melanie's child, subject to being held in trust until she attained at least age 30.

In the event that funds were needed by Melanie prior to Ronald's death, a recommendation might be that an irrevocable inter vivos trust be established to provide for Melanie's welfare, and the bequest passing to Melanie's trust under Ronald's will would be adjusted for equalization with the same amount to be passed to Stephanie or to Stephanie's trust following the administration of Ronald's estate.

c) In selecting an executor for the administration of Ronald's will, I would recommend his wife, Jane Mudd, or his wife, Jane, and his daughter, Stephanie, with consideration as successor executors of Ronald's will, his son, Raoul Mudd, and/or a North Carolina bank or trust company.

In the selection of a trustee for the QTIP marital trust, my recommendations would be Stephanie and/or Raoul with a North Carolina bank or trust company as either a co-trustee or a successor-trustee of the QTIP Trust.

With regard to the naming of a trustee for Melanie's trust, I would certainly consider recommending a California bank if the trust were to be established prior to the death of Ronald Mudd and possibly a California bank (if such bank qualifies to serve as a trustee of a testamentary trust under North Carolina law) as trustee of any testamentary trust established for the benefit of Melanie Mudd and her daughter.

Step 5: Pilot the Test Items and Instructions and Assess Item Quality

Once the requisite number of items have been written, they should be reviewed by all committee members for clarity, relevance, and appropriateness. A sample test form should be created that can include extra items but follows a specified format such as those identified in Step 3. Directions for the exam must be assembled and edited. A pilot form should be created. Each committee member should "take" the test under the specified conditions. Any editing changes should be noted and corrected on the pilot form.

A group of seven to ten individuals recognized by the exam committee members and the bar association as leaders in this specialty should be identified and constitute the pilot test examinees. The pilot test should then be administered under the exact same conditions as the "real" examination. Examinees are asked to note any ambiguities, grammatical errors, and so on that they notice in the test or the directions and the items. These tests should be scored and performance on each item should be noted and compared to committee expectations. This information, in concert with any editing notes from the pilot examinees, should enable the committee members to do one last edit of the items and instructions.

Step 6: Standard Setting

There are several procedures for establishing the cut score on a new test that are recommended in the *Standards for Educational and Psychological Testing* (APA, AERA & NCME, 2014). Two of the most popular methods for setting standards are the modified Angoff method (Angoff, 1971) and the bookmark method (Mitzel et al., 2001). The Angoff method involves having a panel of content specialists evaluate and rate the apparent difficulty of individual items for examinees who are "just qualified." Statistical procedures are then applied to convert the panelists' ratings to a cut score on the score scale. The bookmark method has gained popularity due to its simplicity. The method capitalizes on what is termed "item mapping," where the cut score is directly aligned to the content of a difficulty-ordered collection of test items known as an ordered-item booklet (OIB). That is, using the item proportion-correct values (i.e., item p-values), the *easiest* item (i.e., the item with the greatest p-value) would be placed first and the *most difficult* item (i.e., the item with the lowest p-value) would be placed last.

A standard-setting panel, in this case, the specialty committee members, sets the cut score. The panel is provided with extensive information and training on the bookmark method. In addition, it is recommended that the panelists take the actual test so that they can fully appreciate the difficulty of the items without access to answer keys, supporting documents, and so on.

In addition to an OIB, participants are given an item map. This is a table where each row represents an item in the OIB. Additional information is provided, such as where the item appears on the actual test, the content classification, the p-value (proportion correct, if available) of the item, and a space for the participant's notes.

Following introductory comments, the committee undergoes training and a discussion of what it means to be minimally competent on the examination. During these discussions, panelists express their viewpoints while listening to differing opinions from other panelists. The panelists are then provided with materials and allowed to do a brief training about how the bookmark method works. Following the training, the panelists go through three rounds of ratings, with actionable feedback provided between the rounds. This process should be viewed as a consensus-building exercise.

Using the OIB and the item map, the committee members review the items and discuss the knowledge, skills, and abilities that examinees need to successfully answer the items. Discussion should focus on the features that make the items progressively more difficult. Items can be compared to one another in terms of content and skills that must be mastered for each successively more difficult item. The focus should be on the skills a given item requires for mastery. At the end of Round 1, each committee member ***independently*** places a "bookmark" at the point where they feel borderline test takers would be expected to ***master the items below the bookmark*** and ***not to have mastered the items***

above the bookmark. Figure 3.2 shows the ordered progression of the item by difficulty and placement of the bookmark. The bookmark placement should not be thought of as dividing two items but rather two groups of items. Specifically, examinees whose performance matches a cut score (a minimally qualified examinee) should have about a 2/3 chance of responding correctly to an item at the bookmark location. These same students will have a higher probability of success on easier items (before the bookmark placement) and a lower probability of success on more difficult items (after the bookmark placement).

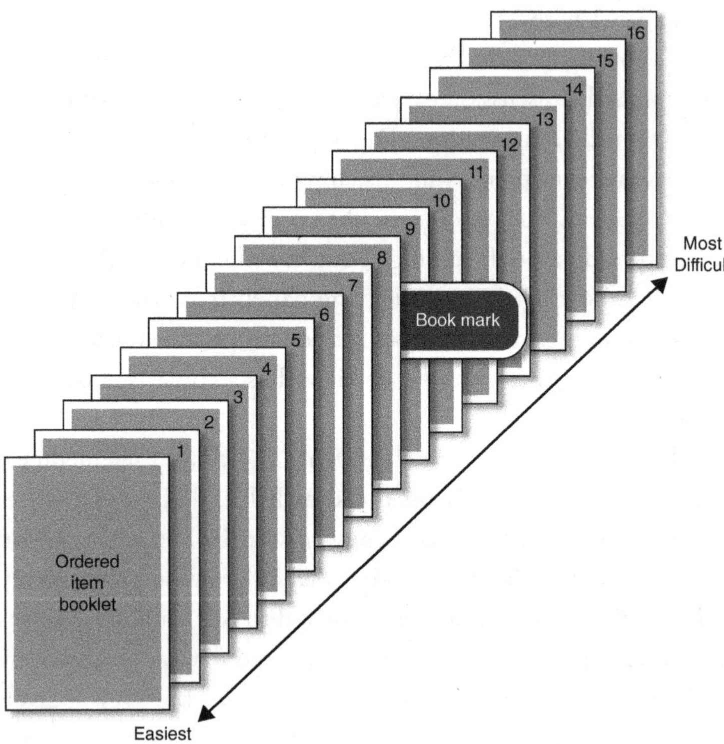

Figure 3.2 The Bookmark Procedure

Round 2

Committee members are provided with everyone's cut score. Members should offer their rationale for the location of their bookmark. Discussion should only focus on the content and necessary skills in the range of the bookmark placements. After hearing the discussion, each member again independently selects a location for their bookmark. They may adjust the location or keep the bookmark in the same location.

Round 3

This round begins with an explanation of the median bookmark location from Round 2. This can be converted to a cut score by simply counting the number of items below the median bookmark location. Impact information related to this cut score is provided. Impact information could include the proportion of examinees who would pass with this cut score, as well as the expected performance of identifiable subgroups of potential concern (e.g., gender, law school attended, city of practice, etc.).

There should also be a group discussion and articulation of the performance level needed to be above the cut score—that is, the committee should develop a performance level descriptor that clarifies the content and skills (as measured by the test) that candidates must demonstrate to pass the exam.

Round 3 concludes with each member independently making their final bookmark placement. The final cut score is based on the median of Round 3's bookmark locations.

One important note from the *Standards for Educational and Psychological Testing* requires that "the level of performance for passing a credentialing test should depend on the knowledge and skills necessary for acceptable performance in the occupation or profession—that is, be criterion-referenced to the content of the test—and should not be adjusted to regulate the number or proportion of persons passing the test."

Step 7: Administering and Scoring the Test

The specialty exam is a standardized test. This means that all examinees will take the test under the exact same conditions using the same directions and time limits. All tests will be scored in the same manner, and all examinees will receive their results in the same format. If the test is computerized, then the type of computer and software used in the administration must be the same, or meet the same specifications, for each examinee. During COVID, computer software was developed to monitor examinees taking a test on the computer for at-home administrations.

It is important that examinees be given information about the material that the exam will cover, the format of the exam (e.g., types and number of questions, length of exam, study guides with potentially released items from former administrations, etc.), how the exam will be administered, and what corresponding materials will be provided. In analogical terms, think of a runner preparing for a race. Due diligence requires that examinees be given the "distance and conditions" of the race they are about to run, so they can train properly. One would train quite differently for a 100-meter dash than for a marathon.

Several testing companies can be used to administer and score specialty exams, including Pearson VUE, Professional Testing Inc., PSI (Psychological Services, Inc.), ExamSoft, and DEKRA SE. These companies will also help in maintaining item pools. It is strongly recommended that bar associations that offer specialty exams should partner with a testing company to not only help maintain the item pool, but also help in computing the test results and corresponding item and test statistics.

Short answer and essay questions are usually scored by the exam committee members, following the established rubrics. At least two members should grade each of these items. If there is a large discrepancy between the two graders, a third grader should be brought in to resolve the difference and assign a final score.

All examinees should be able to see their results in a timely fashion. It is recommended that each examinee receive a score sheet so that they can see how their final score was determined. There should also be an adjudication process should an examinee challenge the test results. Here is an example of a score sheet used for the Trademark Specialty Exam in North Carolina:

Board of Legal Specialization
Individual Grading Report

Exam number: ____________

Specialty area: TRADEMARK

Session 1 score: ______ out of __110__ possible points

Session 2 score: ______ out of __120__ possible points

Session 3 score: ______ out of __135__ possible points

Session 4 score: ______ out of __135__ possible points

Total score: ______ out of __500__ possible points

Cut score/passing score: __74%__ or __370__ possible points

Circle: PASS or FAIL*

FIGURE 3.3 An example score sheet for the North Carolina Trademark Specialty Exam.

Step 8: Analyzing the Test Results

There are many approaches to summarizing the results at both the item and the test level. In this section, we will focus on statistics used in classical test theory (Allen & Yen, 2002). Usually, there are not enough examinees to use more advanced modeling techniques such as item response theory that require at least 200 examinees or more. One key overarching concept is validity. Validity is the degree to which evidence and theory support the interpretations of test scores and the use of examinees' scores on the test. Types of validity include construct, content, face, and criterion related. The most appropriate type for legal specialization exams is content validity. Content validity ensures that the test covers all relevant aspects of the specialty practice. Evidence of content validity is provided in the test specifications, which list the content being measured and the types of items that will be used to measure it. Test validity also requires that the purported skills and competencies that a test is measuring be reliable, or accurately measured. Reliability is discussed later.

Item Statistics

As mentioned earlier, it is strongly recommended that bar associations that offer specialty exams partner with a testing company to help score the multiple-choice portion of the test and compute item statistics, test statistics, and test reliability, discussed next.

Two key statistics that indicate the quality of a test item are difficulty and discrimination. The difficulty of an item is summarized in terms of a p-value. The p-value is simply the proportion of examinees who got the item correct. For example, Table 3.2 shows the results for three items each having four options.

Item	A	B	C	D
1	0	4	15*	4
2	10	14*	3	1
3	2	23*	0	0

*Correct answer

TABLE 3.2 Response data for three items.

The p-values are for Item 1, p = 15/23 = .65; for Item 2, p = 14/28 = .50; and for Item 3, p = 23/25 = .92. P-values range from 0 (no one answered correctly) to 1.0 (everyone answered correctly). A rule of thumb is that p-values should ideally be between .20 and .80. Items that fall out of this range should be edited or replaced. For short answer and essay items, the metric is different, as the difficulty of an essay item would be the average number of points awarded to all of the examinees.

The second quality of an item is discrimination. Effective items are designed to distinguish (i.e., discriminate) between levels of proficiency or understanding. Distractors (wrong alternatives) are designed to attract examinees who lack understanding or have misconceptions. Ideally, all distractors will attract some examinees, although not always. Note in Table 3.2, Distractor A for Item 1 did not attract any examinees. Similarly, no examinees chose Distractors C and D in Item 3. To improve the discrimination quality of an item, distractors that do not have any responses should be examined to see if they can be rephrased.

The statistic that is commonly used to measure the discrimination of an item is called the point biserial correlation (r_{pbis}). It is the Pearson correlation between how examinees scored on an item (usually 0/1, incorrect/correct) and the total scores of the examinees with that item removed. Consider Table 3.3, which indicates the correct (1) or incorrect (0) responses of four examinees to three items. The total score for each examinee is listed in the second-from-right column.

Examinee	Item 1	Item 2	Item 3	Total Score	Total Score with Item 1 removed
1	1	1	1	3	2
2	0	0	1	1	1
3	1	0	1	2	1
4	1	1	0	2	1
r_{pbis}	**–.58**	**.33**	**–.52**		

Table 3.3 Scored responses of four examinees to three items, examinees' total scores, and the r_{pbis} for each item.

The r_{pbs} value for *Item 1* is the correlation between the values 1,0,1,1 with 2,1,1,1 using the formula:

$$r_{pbis} = \frac{n(\sum xy) - (\sum x)(\sum y)}{\sqrt{([n\sum x^2 - (\sum x)^2][n\sum y^2 - (\sum y)^2]}},$$

where r_{pbis} = the point-biserial correlation;

n = the number of items;

$\sum xy$ = the sum of the product of the 0/1 score on the item and the total score with that item's score removed;

$\sum x$ = the sum of the 0/1 scores on the item of interest;

$\sum y$ = the sum of the total scores with the item scores from the item of interest removed;

$\sum x^2$ = the sum of the item 0/1 scores each squared;

$\sum y^2$ = the sum of the total scores with the item of interest score removed each squared;

$(\sum x)^2$ = the sum of the 0/1 item scores the quantity scored;

$(\sum y)^2$ = the sum of the total scores with the item scores from the item of interest removed, the quantity squared.

For Item 1 the calculations are as follows:

$$r_{pbis} = \frac{n(\sum xy) - (\sum x)(\sum y)}{\sqrt{([n\sum x^2 - (\sum x)^2][n\sum y^2 - (\sum y)^2]}}$$

$$= \frac{4(4) - (3)(6)}{\sqrt{[4(3) - 9][4(10) - 36]}} = \frac{-2}{3.464} = -.58$$

The value of r_{pbis} ranges from –1 to +1. Guidelines for interpreting the value of this statistic are as follows:

- Very Good Item: .30 and above
- Reasonably Good Item: .20–.29
- Marginal Item: .09–.19
- Poor Item: below .09

Negative values mean that examinees with high scores tended to get this item wrong and examinees with low scores tended to get this item correct. High negative values could indicate that the item was miskeyed. Note also that with a small number of examinees, the statistic is not very stable, and values can fluctuate widely. For short answer and essay items, the calculation of r_{pbis} is the same as with a multiple-choice item.

After every administration, the p-value and r_{pbis} for each item should be checked, and items that fall out of the acceptable range for each statistic should be reviewed and possibly edited for improvement.

Total Score Statistics

At the total test score level, several statistics are calculated: the mean, the standard deviation, the reliability, and the standard error of measurement. The mean is simply the numerical average of all the test scores. Note that there are several types of averages, including the median (the score that separates the 50 percent of scores above and below it) and the mode (the score that occurs most frequently). The median and mean do not have to be an observed value. It is also important to look at a distribution of the scores to determine if the distribution is symmetric, positively skewed, or negatively skewed. In Figure 3.4, the three types of distributional shapes are displayed along with the position of the three types of averages.

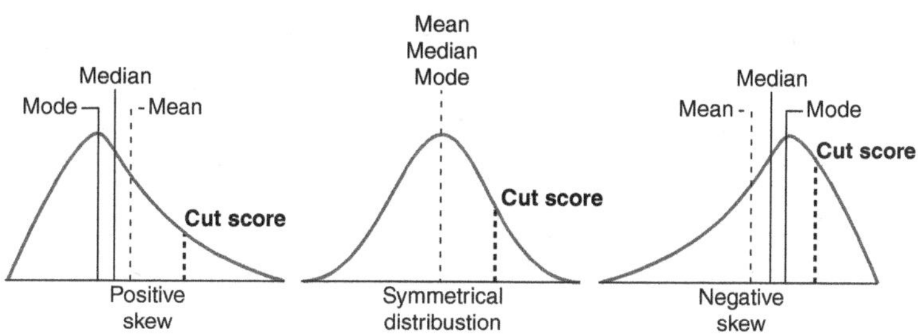

FIGURE 3.4 Distributional shapes and types of averages for a set of test scores.

A positively skewed distribution represents a "difficult" test, and a negatively skewed distribution represents an "easy" test. Also graphed on the distribution of scores should be the cut score. The proportion of area above the cut score represents the proportion of examinees who passed the test.

The standard deviation is a statistic that indicates the spread of the scores. It is usually denoted as S (indicating you are working with a sample) or σ (indicating you are working with a population). The formula is as follows:

$$S = \sqrt{\frac{\Sigma x^2 - \frac{(\Sigma x)^2}{N}}{N - 1}},$$

where S = the standard deviation;

$(\Sigma x)^2$ = the sum of the total scores (*X*s), the quantity squared;

Σx^2 = the sum of each total score squared; and

N = the number of examinees.

The standard deviation of the total scores in Table 3.3 is

$$S = \sqrt{\frac{\Sigma x^2 - \frac{(\Sigma x)^2}{N}}{N - 1}} = \sqrt{\frac{18 - \frac{64}{4}}{4 - 1}} = \sqrt{\frac{2}{3}} = .816$$

The standard deviation is actually the square root of what is called the variance (S^2). The problem is that the variance is in squared units, so to put the statistic back on the raw score metric, we take the square root. Because the standard deviation is a square root, it can never be negative, but it can equal zero if everyone achieves the same total score. A crude (but NOT EXACT) interpretation is that S indicates how much on average each examinee differs from the mean. The larger the standard deviation, the greater the spread of scores.

It is best to look at the total score statistics for each type of item separately, as the total possible scores will vary by type.

The last statistic is the reliability. There are many formulas for reliability, but in this chapter the focus will be on one of the most commonly used reliability coefficients, KR-20. Technically reliability is defined as the ratio of

$$\text{KR-20} = \frac{\sigma^2_{\text{True Score}}}{\sigma^2_X}$$

where $\sigma^2_{\text{True Score}}$ is the variance of hypothetical true scores, scores the examinees would obtain if there were no measurement error, and is the variance of the observed total scores. Observed scores are thought to have two components, the individual's true score and measurement error. Measurement error is another theoretical construct that is thought to be **random** missteps of an examinee. Error scores would vary from examinee to examinee. Both true scores and error scores are unobservable. If there is no measurement error (an impossible result), the reliability would be 1.0. Since reliability is a theoretical construct, we must make assumptions and estimate it. The assumptions are beyond the scope of this chapter. The formula that is used quite often is KR-20 (Kuder Richardson formula 20), a common measure of *internal consistency* of a test when items are dichotomously scored: 0 = incorrect, 1 = correct. Usually, as the number of items increases, reliability will increase. Acceptable values are usually in the range of .75 or higher. For a frame of reference, standardized college admissions tests (e.g., ACT, SAT, GRE) tend to be in the low .90s. Items that measure different contents (e.g., multidimensionality) and low (or negative) point biserials can lower reliability. The formula is given as

$$\text{KR-20} = \frac{n}{n-1}\left[1 - \frac{\Sigma\sigma^2_{\text{Item}}}{\sigma^2_X}\right]$$

where n is the number of items, $\sum\sigma^2_{\text{Item}}$ is the sum of the individual item variances, and σ^2_X is the sum of the variance of the total scores.

The number of examinees does not enter into the calculation of KR-20, although the more examinees, the more stable the reliability. This measure should be used with multiple-choice items primarily.

The standard error of measurement (SEM) is a measure of the precision of the test. It is calculated using the reliability: SEM $= \sigma\sqrt{1 - \text{reliability}}$. The greater the reliability (the more "internally consistent" the test), the lower the value of the SEM. The SEM is used to set a confidence interval (CI) about a test score.

For example, to create a 90 percent CI about a test score of, say, 75 with an SEM of 3.6, we would use the formula 90% CI = x +/– 1.645(SEM):

$$\text{Lower limit: } 75 - 1.645(3.6) = 69.08$$

$$\text{Upper limit: } 75 + 1.645(3.6) = 80.92$$

What this means is that we know our test has measurement error, and thus if this examinee were to test 100 times independently, we would be confident that 90 percent of their scores would be between 69.08 and 80.92. The higher the reliability, the smaller the SEM and the narrower the confidence interval and thus the more accurate the test score.

Step 9: Maintenance

Creating and maintaining a specialty exam is always a work in progress. Every year the specialty committee should strive to improve their test. Specialty areas are never static but are constantly changing, some more quickly than others. It is imperative that the exam be current and reflect the day-to-day activities of the specialty. About every five years lawyers in a specialty area should be surveyed to ensure the content being measured is current (Raymond, 2001). Depending upon the rate of change in a specialty area, such analyses may need to be more frequent.

It is necessary to reiterate that documentation is essential. Every decision a committee makes, and the corresponding rationale, needs to be documented in a "living" technical manual. The benefits of documentation and alignment with the *Standards for Educational and Psychological Testing* (APA, AERA & NCME, 2014) are threefold. Documentation provides for

1. **Clarity and Understanding:**
   - Documentation acts as a guide, providing a clear understanding of procedures, decisions, and supporting rationales.
   - Recording committee decisions ensures transparency and helps new members understand past choices.
2. **Collaboration and Accountability:**
   - Well-documented test construction, scoring, and exam administration details serve as a central repository of information, fostering collaboration among team members.
   - When examinees challenge exam results, having documented decisions provides evidence and accountability.
3. **Risk Reduction and Consistency:**
   - Detailed documentation reduces confusion and minimizes errors.
   - Adhering to standards ensures consistent practices and reliable and valid outcomes.

Remember, technical documentation empowers stakeholders by making information accessible and understandable. It is an investment that will pay off in transparency, efficiency, and trust.

References

Allen, M. J., & Yen, W. M. (2002). *Introduction to measurement theory*. Long Grove, IL: Waveland Press.

American Psychological Association, American Educational Research Association & National Council on Measurement in Education (Eds.). (2014). *Standards for educational and psychological testing*. American Educational Research Association.

Angoff, W. H. (1971). Test scores and norms. In L. C. Deighton (Ed.), *Encyclopedia of Education* (pp. 153–165). New York: Macmillan.

Bloom, B. S. (1956). *Taxonomy of educational objectives, handbook I: The cognitive domain*. New York: David McKay Co. Inc.

Case, S., & Swanson, D. (2003). *Constructing written test questions for the basic and clinical sciences*. Philadelphia, PA: National Board of Medical Examiners (available online).

Haladyna, T. M. (2004). *Developing and validating multiple-choice test items* (3rd ed.). Lawrence Erlbaum Associates Publishers.

Haladyna, T., & Rodriguez, M. C. (2013). *Developing and validating test items*. New York: Taylor-Francis/Routledge.

Luecht, R. M. (2017). Professional certification and licensure examinations. In A. A. Rupp & J. P. Leighton (Eds.), *The handbook of cognition and assessment: Frameworks, methodologies, and applications* (pp. 446–471). New York: Wiley.

Mitzel, H. C., Lewis, D. M., Patz, R. J., & Green, D. R. (2001). The bookmark procedure: Psychological perspectives. In G. J. Cizek (Ed.), *Setting performance standards: Concepts, methods, and perspectives* (pp. 249–281). Lawrence Erlbaum Associates Publishers.

Mullen, D. (2024). The North Carolina State Bar Board of Legal Specialization Exam Manual.

Raymond, M. R. (2001). Job analysis and the specification of content for licensure and certification examinations. *Applied Measurement in Education, 14*, 369–415.

Raymond, M. R., & Luecht, R. M. (2013). Licensure and certification testing. In K. F. Geisinger, B. A. Bracken, J. F. Carlson, J.-I. C. Hansen, N. R. Kuncel, S. P. Reise, & M. C. Rodriguez (Eds.), *APA handbook of testing and assessment in psychology, Vol. 3. Testing and assessment in school psychology and education* (pp. 391–414). American Psychological Association. https://doi.org/10.1037/14049-019.

Raymond, M. R., & Neustel, S. (2006). Determining the content of credentialing examinations. In S. M. Downing & T. M. Haladyna (Eds.), *Handbook of test development* (pp. 181–223). Mahwah, NJ: Lawrence Erlbaum Associates.

Webb, N. (1997). Research monograph no. 6. Criteria for alignment of expectations and assessments on mathematics and science education. Washington, DC: CCSSO.

Appendix A

Glossary

Correlation: Refers to the relationship between two or more variables (i.e., the extent to which they vary together). The most commonly used measure of correlation, Pearson's correlation coefficient, ranges from –1 to 1, with 0 indicating no relationship. Positive correlations imply measures on two variables increase together. Negative correlations imply that as one variable increases, the other decreases.

Distractor: For a multiple-choice test question, distractor response options are all the options except the correct choice. They "distract" the examinee from the correct answer.

Item Difficulty (p, p-value): Represents the percentage of examinees answering the item correctly and is estimated by the p-value for the correct answer choice. P-values can range from 0 to 1. Values near 0 indicate that few examinees in the sample selected the correct answer choice (the item was difficult). Values near 1 indicate that most examinees selected the correct answer choice (the item was easy).

Item Discrimination: Represents the extent to which the item differentiated between examinees of different abilities (lower and higher) related to the knowledge and/or skills assessed on the exam. For dichotomous items, item discrimination is estimated as point biserial correlations. See Correlation, Point Biserial Correlation.

KR-20: An estimate of reliability. KR-20 can be conceptualized as internal consistency—the degree to which all test items measure the same underlying proficiency or trait. Values range from 0 to 1, where values closer to 1 indicate greater consistency.

Values greater than .80 are typically considered sufficient for certification examinations. See Reliability.

Kurtosis: The peakedness or flatness of the frequency distribution. In this formulation a normal curve would have a kurtosis value of 0.

Mean: A measure of the central tendency of the data. Determined by adding up all values in the data and dividing the sum by the number of observations.

Median: A numerical type of average, below which lie 50 percent of the examinees' scores and above which lie 50 percent of the examinees' scores. It does not have to be an observed score.

Mode: A type of average. It is the observed score that occurs most often. It does not have to lie in the middle of the score distribution.

Normal Distribution or Normality: A probability distribution where values with higher probabilities of occurrence are concentrated around the mean, deviating from the mean as their probability of occurrence decreases. A normal distribution has a distinct bell-shaped curve.

Point Biserial Correlation: A measure of item discrimination. Refers to the correlation between the total scores of examinees and their scores on a particular item. Values range from –1 to 1. Items with values below .15 are typically flagged for review or removal. Note that the biserial for distractors should be negative! See Item Discrimination, Correlation.

P-value: Proportion of examinees who answer an item correctly. See Item Difficulty.

Reliability: The degree to which examinee scores are consistent across items, versions of assessments, or occasions. Measures of reliability indicate the internal consistency, stability, or precision of the performance scale.

Skewness: A measure of symmetry. A perfectly symmetrical distribution (e.g., a normal distribution) would have a skewness value of 0.

Standard Deviation (s): A measure of the extent to which scores vary around their mean.

Standard Error of Measurement (SEM): Refers to the extent examinee scores might change across items, assessment versions, or testing occasions. It is used to show the amount of error likely associated with an examinee's observed score.

Chapter 4

Ethical Considerations in Seeking, Maintaining, and Advertising Legal Specialization

Carolyn A. Dubay[1]

Introduction

Lawyers who specialize in a field of law must be mindful of several key ethical considerations either when seeking and maintaining status as a legal specialist or when holding themselves out as a legal specialist without certification. This chapter provides an overview of three key issues in this area: (1) advertising as a legal specialist, either with or without certification; (2) the duty of care owed by those who hold themselves out as legal specialists; and (3) other ethical considerations in seeking and maintaining certification as a legal specialist, including information for judges who wish to maintain or gain certification while in judicial service. For

1. Chief Counsel, Rules Committee Staff, Administrative Office of the U.S. Courts. Note that this chapter represents only the personal views, opinions, research, and perspective of the author. Ms. Dubay is a member of the Judicial Division's Ethics and Professionalism Committee. She is past chair of the Lawyers Conference of the ABA Judicial Division and has chaired various committees within the Judicial Division, including its Program Committee and Model Law Clerk Code of Conduct Working Group. Ms. Dubay has also served as a special advisor to the Judges Committee of the ABA Standing Committee on Ethics and Professional Responsibility.

purposes of this chapter, reference is made to the ABA's *Model Rules of Professional Conduct* (ABA Model Rules) adopted in 1983, as amended,[2] and the ABA *Model Code of Judicial Conduct.*[3] Because ethical rules and disciplinary authority governing lawyer conduct differ from state to state, lawyers and judges should always refer to their applicable codes of conduct and contact ethics advisory officials regarding specific application of these rules.

As set forth in this chapter, once a lawyer obtains certification as a legal specialist, due care must be given to how that specialization status is advertised or communicated. For lawyers who specialize in a certain area but do not have certification, there are also very specific rules as to how that specialization can be denoted publicly. For lawyers who are certified as a legal specialist, depending on the entity that granted the certification, there may also be detailed rules regarding the disclosures that must accompany any public statement as to the certification. This is an area where there is a tremendous amount of regulatory variation state to state that must be carefully considered.

Attorneys should also consider whether their state recognizes a heightened duty of care toward clients once legal specialist status is obtained—whether by certification or otherwise. Traditional notions of attorney competence—once based on the ideal of the generalist attorney—have been challenged as lawyers increasingly seek legal certification or develop a specialization to maintain competitiveness. In this new landscape, while the ethical duty of competence continues to allow nonspecialists to handle cases, courts evaluating legal malpractice claims have recognized a

---

2. Available on the ABA's website at https://www.americanbar.org/groups/professional_responsibility/publications/model_rules_of_professional_conduct (last visited Apr. 22, 2025).

3. Available on the ABA's website at https://www.americanbar.org/groups/professional_responsibility/publications/model_code_of_judicial_conduct (last visited Apr. 22, 2025).

specialist duty of care that evaluates the lawyer's handling of a case based on the actions of a similarly situated legal specialist.

Finally, beyond these issues, the legal specialization process itself raises new ethical concerns that may arise during the process of obtaining, and then maintaining, the status of a legal specialist. This includes ethical issues not only for lawyers but also for judges who are asked to provide references as part of the certification process or who wish to pursue or maintain legal specialist status while on the bench.

Advertising a Legal Specialization: Ethical and Constitutional Considerations

The issue of attorney advertising—one that involves both regulatory and constitutional dimensions—has produced a number of thorny issues about how far state regulators can go in (1) ensuring that a lawyer who advertises their certification as a legal specialist does so in a manner that is not false or misleading and (2) ensuring that a lawyer who does not have a certification (from either a state or an accredited private program) does not advertise their specialization in a manner that could imply recognition by an independent entity as a specialist. Although the ABA Model Rules include a model rule relating to advertising specialist status, this is an area where the adopted rules in each state vary greatly. Lawyers should therefore consult their applicable state rule when considering how to denote legal specialist status on everything from letterhead to advertisements.

The ABA has addressed the ethical issues involved in developing a legal specialty for nearly a hundred years. The ABA's first code of conduct for lawyers—the 1908 *Canons of Professional Ethics*—addressed legal specialization for the first time in 1928 through adoption of Canon 45, which made clear that legal specialists were subject to the same standards of conduct as practitioners who did not hold themselves out as legal specialists.[4] At the time, the Canons also contained a strict prohibition on attorney advertising, whether as a specialist or otherwise. The Canons were amended in 1933, however, to include a limited provision to allow attorneys who practiced in specialized areas to advertise their expertise, but only in communications to other lawyers. Under Canon 46, "lawyers undertaking specialized legal work exclusively for other lawyers" were permitted to "advertise such specialized legal work in a 'dignified' manner in legal periodicals."[5]

In the decades that followed, legal specialization continued to grow, and the ABA began to consider whether and how lawyers could note their specialty beyond lawyer-to-lawyer advertisements. As a first step, in 1951, the ABA amended Canon 27, which governed lawyer advertising in general, and permitted lawyers to note their legal specialty on their letterhead.[6] The next year, the ABA amended Canon 27 again, this time to allow admiralty and patent lawyers (long-recognized legal specialties) to state their specialties on their "shingles."[7]

---

4. *See* Michael Ariens, *Know the Law: A History of Legal Specialization*, 45 S.C. L. Rev. 1003, 1035 (1994). *See also* American Bar Association, *Canons of Professional Ethics*, 27 N.D. L. Rev. 243, 259 (1951), available at https://commons.und.edu/ndlr/vol27/iss2/14 (last visited Apr. 22, 2025) [hereinafter Canons] (quoting Canon 45: "The canons of the American Bar Association apply to all branches of the legal profession; specialists in particular branches are not to be considered as exempt from the application of these principles.").

5. *See* Ariens, *supra* note 4, at 1035. *See also* Canons, *supra* note 4, at 25 (quoting Canon 46: "Where a lawyer is engaged in rendering a specialized legal service directly and only to other lawyers, a brief, dignified notice of that fact, couched in language indicating that it is addressed to lawyers, inserted in legal periodicals and like publications, when it will afford convenient and beneficial information to lawyers desiring to obtain such service, is not improper.").

6. Ariens, *supra* note 4, at 1042.

7. *See* Michael S. Ariens, *Sorting: Legal Specialization and the Privatization of the American Legal Profession*, 29 Geo. J. Legal Ethics 579, 583 (2016) ("[T]he ABA began a halting effort to recognize the existence of traditional

In 1969, the ABA replaced the Canons with the *Model Code of Professional Responsibility* (ABA Model Code).[8] The ABA Model Code still prohibited attorney advertising but carried over Canon 27's provision allowing lawyers practicing in the fields of admiralty, trademark, and patent law to advertise that specialty.[9] Thereafter, however, the ABA made major amendments to the ABA Model Code to address the issue of attorney advertising, both generally and in the specific context of legal specialization. Two developments necessitated this focus. First, the U.S. Supreme Court issued its landmark decision in *Bates v. State Bar of Arizona*[10] in 1977, which involved a challenge to an Arizona rule prohibiting lawyers from advertising their rates for certain routine services.[11] In *Bates*, the Supreme Court recognized lawyer advertising as constitutionally protected commercial speech under the First Amendment and invalidated long-standing bans on legal advertising as long as the information conveyed was not false or misleading.[12] Second, the ABA Model Code had to address the advent of state certification programs for legal specialties, which

---

legal specialists. It amended Canon 27 of its 1908 Canons of Ethics by allowing patent and admiralty lawyers to indicate on letterhead their specialties.").

8. The ABA Model Code is available at https://www.americanbar.org/content/dam/aba/administrative/professional_responsibility/model-code-of-prof-responsibility1969.pdf (last visited Apr. 22, 2025).

9. EC 2-14 provided as follows: "In the absence of state controls to insure the existence of special competence, a lawyer should not be permitted to hold himself out as a specialist or as having official recognition as a specialist, other than in the fields of admiralty, trademark, and patent law where a holding out as a specialist historically has been permitted."

10. 433 U.S. 350 (1977).

11. The opinion in *Bates* made clear that it was limited in scope to the regulation of attorney advertising and only as to concrete factual issues such as rates. Its decision did not extend to restrictions on statements as to the quality of services or restrictions on in-person solicitation of clients (particularly in hospitals or other contexts where undue influence might arise). *See id.* at 366.

12. *See id.* at 383.

began in California and Texas in the early 1970s.[13] With this innovation, lawyers wanted to be able to advertise that not only did they practice in a specialized area but an independent entity had also certified them as a legal specialist.

In light of these developments, the ABA Model Code ultimately contained several provisions—both ethical considerations [ECs] and disciplinary rules [DRs]—relating to advertising legal specialist status. Under EC 2-10, a lawyer generally could communicate (e.g., advertise) their "education, experience or professional qualifications" but had to "avoid the use of any statement or claim which is false, fraudulent, misleading, deceptive or unfair, or which is violative of any statute or rule of court."[14] Specific guidance relating to advertising and communicating about a legal specialty was set forth in EC 2-14.[15] First, in states that did not have a legal specialization program, the traditional rule remained in place that only practitioners in admiralty, patent, and trademark law could hold themselves out as legal specialists.[16] Other lawyers could note, however, that they restricted their practice to certain areas.[17] Second, for lawyers who practiced in jurisdictions that did offer certification programs, EC 2-14 focused on ensuring that lawyers without certification as a legal specialist did not advertise in a way that implied they had a certification as a specialist. Specifically, under EC 2-14, if a lawyer "discloses areas of law in which he practices or to which he limits his practice, but is not certified in [the jurisdiction], he . . . should avoid any

---

13. *See* Ariens, *supra* note 4, at 1054. Under DR 2-105(A), a lawyer or law firm could "publicly identify one or more areas of law in which the lawyer or the law firm practices, or may state that the practice of the lawyer or law firm is limited to one or more areas of law." *See* ABA Model Code, *supra* note 8.

14. *See* ABA Model Code, *supra* note 8, EC 2-10.

15. *See id.*, EC 2-14.

16. *Id.*

17. *Id.*

implication that he is in fact certified."[18] As to how certified legal specialists could advertise their status, under DR 2-105(B), the ABA Model Code deferred to the rules established by the state certifying board or authority.[19]

In 1983, the ABA Model Code was replaced by the ABA *Model Rules of Professional Conduct* (the ABA Model Rules), which, after a major revision in 2000, have been the model for all 50 states and the District of Columbia.[20] Like the ABA Model Code, the ABA Model Rules provided scant specific rules for legal specialists, with a continued focus exclusively on advertising. This focus was driven by the proliferation of legal specialist programs throughout the 1980s and 1990s, some sponsored by state bars and others by private entities, and the desire of states to protect the public from false or misleading advertising regarding certification from unregulated private entities.[21]

With respect to advertising certification from a private entity, many states initially took a hard line with lawyers who held themselves out as a certified legal specialist unless the certification was

---

18. *Id.*

19. *See id.*, DR 2-105(B). Similarly, under EC 2-14, lawyers practicing in a limited or specialized area could designate that fact in advertising, so long as the lawyer used the "designations and definitions authorized" by the appropriate state authority. EC 2-14 also provided that a lawyer could "indicate in permitted advertising, if it is factual, a limitation of his practice or one or more particular areas or fields of law in which he practices using designations and definitions authorized for that purpose by [the state agency having jurisdiction]."

20. *See* ABA Model Rules, *supra* note 2. In 2000, through recommendations of the ABA's Ethics 2000 Commission, the Model Rules were revised significantly to address, among other issues, the need for greater uniformity among the 44 states that used the Model Rules at the time. The ABA Model Rules were amended most recently in 2023.

21. *Cf.* Buddy O. Herring, *Liability of Board Certified Specialists in a Legal Malpractice Action: Is There a Higher Standard?*, 12 Geo. J. Legal Ethics 67, 73–74 (1998) (describing interaction of ABA efforts to develop standards for certification and legal challenges to restrictions on lawyer advertising of certification status).

granted by a government entity. The restrictive approach led to another landmark challenge to the constitutionality of state regulations governing lawyer advertising. In *Peel v. Attorney Registration and Disciplinary Commission of Illinois,*[22] the U.S. Supreme Court confronted the issue of a lawyer—Gary Peel—who was sanctioned by the Illinois Supreme Court for violating a court-adopted rule of professional conduct that prohibited advertising as a legal specialist unless the state had issued the certification. Peel, who was certified as a specialist by the National Board of Trial Advocacy (NBTA) and not a state certifying authority, argued that his advertising was factual and not misleading and therefore constitutionally protected.

Based on its review of the record, the U.S. Supreme Court agreed with Peel and concluded that because nothing in the language of the advertisement could cause confusion as to the granting organization (i.e., it was not false or misleading) and the NBTA issued certifications based on qualifications rather than payment alone, the advertisement was protected speech under the First Amendment.[23] This decision had a dramatic effect on the development of legal specialist programs by allowing private entities to offer certification, albeit subject to state rules governing advertising specialist status.[24] In fact, while *Peel* was making its way through the courts, the ABA acted to develop standards for offering certification as a legal specialist and procedures for private entities to seek accreditation of their programs.[25]

---

22. 496 U.S. 91 (1990).

23. *See id.* at 100–02.

24. *See* Ariens, *supra* note 4, at 1059–60 (*Peel* "ended the process of bar-controlled certification of specialists" but left open state regulation as to whether "some claims of certification may be considered misleading or may be regulated by the state through required disclaimers").

25. *See* Herring, *supra* note 21, at 73 ("As a further reaction to the Peel decision, states asked the ABA to help in setting standards for accreditation of private certification organizations. Many states were concerned that private

Today, the ABA Model Rules address attorney advertising in general under Model Rule 7.1, which prohibits any "false or misleading communication about the lawyer or the lawyer's services."[26] As explained in Comment 2 to Model Rule 7.1, a misleading statement (including an advertisement) can be one that "omits a fact necessary to make the lawyer's communication considered as a whole not materially misleading."[27] Similarly, a communication is misleading if "a substantial likelihood exists that it will lead a reasonable person to formulate a specific conclusion about the lawyer or the lawyer's services for which there is no reasonable factual foundation."[28]

Model Rule 7.2(c) governs advertising legal specialization status. Lawyers who have been certified by a state or private entity as a legal specialist may advertise that they are certified as a specialist only if the certifying organization has been approved by a government entity or is accredited by the ABA and the name of the certifying organization is "clearly identified" in the advertisement or other communication.[29] For lawyers who do not have a

---

organizations would begin to issue certifications of specialization simply upon the payment of a fee or with little demonstration of competence."). The ABA's current standards are available at https://www.americanbar.org/content/dam/aba/administrative/specialization/aba-standards-for-accreditation-specialization.pdf (last visited Apr. 22, 2025).

26. Model Rule 7.1 provides that a communication is false or misleading if it contains a material misrepresentation of fact or law or omits a fact necessary to make the statement considered as a whole not materially misleading. https://www.americanbar.org/groups/professional_responsibility/publications/model_rules_of_professional_conduct/rule_7_1_communication_concerning_a_lawyer_s_services/ (last visited Apr. 22, 2025).

27. ABA Model Rule 7.1, Comment 2, available at https://www.americanbar.org/groups/professional_responsibility/publications/model_rules_of_professional_conduct/rule_7_1_communication_concerning_a_lawyer_s_services/ (last visited Apr. 22, 2025).

28. *Id.*

29. Model Rule 7.2(c) provides that a "lawyer shall not state or imply that a lawyer is certified as a specialist in a particular field of law, unless: (1) the lawyer

legal certification, or who received one from an entity that does not satisfy Model Rule 7.2(c)(1), their advertising is governed by Model Rule 7.1's general restrictions on false or misleading advertising. The comments to Rule 7.2, however, provide specific guidance on communicating about a legal practice that is limited to a specific field. Under these comments, a lawyer without certification from an accredited or approved entity may not hold themself out as having a certification as a legal specialist but may "communicate that they practice in a particular area and can say that the lawyer 'concentrates in' or is a 'specialist' or practices a 'specialty' based on experience, specialized training or education."[30]

Although Model Rule 7.2(c) attempts to balance the constitutional right of lawyers to advertise their certification as a legal specialist and the need to protect the public from misleading statements about a lawyer's qualifications, any action to discipline an attorney based on advertisement of a certification is subject to First Amendment scrutiny. For example, in 1994, the U.S. Supreme Court in *Ibanez v. Florida Department of Business and Professional Regulation*[31] found that a disciplinary decision by the Florida Board of Accountancy against Ms. Ibanez, a Florida attorney, for denoting her status as both a CPA (certified public accountant) and a CFP (certified financial planner)

---

has been certified as a specialist by an organization that has been approved by an appropriate authority of the state or the District of Columbia or a U.S. Territory or that has been accredited by the American Bar Association; and (2) the name of the certifying organization is clearly identified in the communication." *See* ABA Model Rules, *supra* note 2.

30. *See* Rule 7.2: Communications Concerning a Lawyer's Services: Specific Rules—Comment 9, available at https://www.americanbar.org/groups/professional_responsibility/publications/model_rules_of_professional_conduct/rule_7_2_advertising/comment_on_rule_7_2/ (last visited Apr. 22, 2025) (noting further that "such communications are subject to the 'false and misleading' standard applied in Rule 7.1 to communications concerning a lawyer's services").

31. 512 U.S. 136 (1994).

in public statements was unconstitutional.[32] Although *Ibanez* involved restrictions and sanctions issued by the Florida Board of Accountancy and not the Florida Bar, the Supreme Court specifically addressed the constitutionality of sanctions against professionals for advertising certification status. As in *Peel*, the Supreme Court found that the sanction was an unconstitutional restriction on Ms. Ibanez's free speech because use of the CPA and CFP designations was neither false (she had obtained a certification from a private organization) nor misleading (because consumers could contact the CFP Board of Standards—a private entity—to determine the nature and extent of the designation).[33]

Several years after the Supreme Court's decision in *Ibanez*, another lawyer challenged a sanction imposed for failing to comply with a state disclaimer requirement related to advertising a private certification. In *Hayes v. New York Attorney Grievance Committee*,[34] the U.S. Court of Appeals for the Second Circuit declared unconstitutional a New York rule that required attorneys who identified themselves as certified specialists to make prescribed disclosures regarding the certifying organization through a "prominent" display of disclaimers about the certifying organization.[35] The state rule also went further than the ABA Model Rule and required additional details about the certification. For

32. The Florida Bar was not a party to the case and had not taken action against Ms. Ibanez based on use of the designations of CPA and CFP on her letterhead and other legal advertisements. The State Board of Accounting asserted its disciplinary jurisdiction over Ms. Ibanez based on her status as a CPA and argued that her use of the CPA designation indicated that she practiced as an accountant (which she denied), that her law firm was not a licensed accounting firm, and, further, that her use of the CFP certification did not meet the detailed disclaimer requirements for specialty designations. *See id.* at 139–40.

33. *See id.* at 144–45.

34. 672 F.3d 158 (2d Cir. 2012).

35. *See id.* at 163–64 (further noting that at the time, 48 states had rules that permitted lawyers to identify themselves as specialists and noting various differences among the states).

example, the state rule required a statement that certification is not a requirement for the practice of law and that certification "does not necessarily indicate greater competence than other attorneys experienced in this field of law."[36]

In *Hayes*, there was no dispute that the attorney had received the requisite certification. Instead, the focus was on two issues: whether the detailed disclaimers about the certifying organization unduly burdened protected commercial speech, and whether the requirement that the disclaimers be "prominently made" was unconstitutionally vague. The Second Circuit struck down the New York rule on both grounds. First, as to the requirement of disclaimers in general, the Second Circuit found that there were no constitutional concerns in requiring a disclaimer as to the nature of the certifying organization because of the risk that some members of the public would believe that a government entity had approved the certification of lawyers in their field of specialty.[37] On the other hand, the Second Circuit took issue with the extensiveness of the required disclaimers, finding that in the absence of any evidence of risk to the public or other harm, the extensive disclaimers amounted to an unconstitutional burden on free speech.[38] Second, the court found that the requirement that the disclosures be "prominently made" was unconstitutionally vague.[39] For example, the New York rule failed to provide adequate notice to lawyers as to the required placement and font of the disclaimer when used in different contexts, such as billboards, stationery, business cards, or radio/television ads.[40]

This case law teaches that the devil is in the details on how far a state can go in regulating lawyer advertising of certified

36. *Id.* at 162 (internal quotations omitted).

37. *Id.* at 167.

38. *See id.* at 167–68.

39. *See id.* at 169.

40. *Id.*

legal specialist status. Different states have adopted very different approaches to addressing these concerns. Importantly, some states have more restrictive rules than provided in Model Rule 7.2 and may prevent use of certain language or require fuller disclosures. Lawyers who practice in a specific area, or those who wish to advertise a certification in a legal specialty, should therefore carefully review their state's rules of professional responsibility to determine (1) what language can be used to convey specialization without a certification; (2) if the lawyer is certified as a specialist, whether the granting organization is recognized under the state rule; and (3) the extent of any disclaimers that must also accompany any public statements noting the certification.

Lawyers without a certification as a specialist, or who received a certification from an entity that is not recognized under the state rule, should also be aware that depending on the jurisdiction, there may be specific guidelines on the use of the word "specialist" or other indications that the lawyer "specializes" in a specific field. For example, under Rule 7.4(b) of the California Rules of Professional Conduct, a lawyer with no certification can communicate that their practice "specializes in, is limited to, or is concentrated in a particular field of law," so long as it is not false or misleading.[41] On the other hand, in a more restrictive state,

---

41. Rule 7.4(b) of the California Rules of Professional Conduct is available at https://www.calbar.ca.gov/Portals/0/documents/rules/Rule_7.4-Exec_Summary-Redline.pdfRule_7.4-Exec_Summary-Redline.pdf (last visited Apr. 22, 2025). Rule 7.4(a) governs advertising legal specialist status with a certification:

> (a) A lawyer shall not state that the lawyer is a certified specialist in a particular field of law, unless:
>
> (1) the lawyer is currently certified as a specialist by the Board of Legal Specialization, or any other entity accredited by the State Bar to designate specialists pursuant to standards adopted by the Board of Trustees; and
>
> (2) the name of the certifying organization is clearly identified in the communication.

such as North Carolina, lawyers who lack recognized certification as a specialist but who specialize in an area of the law may not hold themselves out as a "specialist" or state that they "specialize" in a particular practice area.[42] Instead, such lawyers must find other ways to indicate their areas of practice, such as by indicating a "concentration" or a "limitation" in their practice areas.[43] As explained in Comment 7 to Rule 7.2(c) of the North Carolina Rules of Professional Conduct: "The use of the word 'specialize' in any of its variant forms connotes to the public a particular expertise often subject to recognition by the state."[44]

Similarly, under Rule 4-7.14 of the Florida Rules of Professional Conduct, a lawyer may not engage in potentially misleading advertising, which includes "a statement that the lawyer is a specialist or an expert in an area of practice, or other variations of those terms," unless either the lawyer is certified (as permitted under the Florida rules) or "the lawyer can objectively verify the claim based on the lawyer's education, training, experience, or substantial involvement in the area of practice in which specialization or expertise is claimed."[45] As explained in the comments to this rule, a lawyer may state "that the lawyer concentrates in,

---

42. *See* Rule 7.2(c) of the North Carolina Rules of Professional Conduct, available at https://www.ncbar.gov/for-lawyers/ethics/rules-of-professional-conduct/rule-72-rule-72-communications-concerning-a-lawyers-services-specific-rules/ (last visited Apr. 22, 2025). Under North Carolina Rule 7.2(c): "A lawyer shall not state that the lawyer specializes or is a specialist in a field of practice unless: (1) the lawyer is certified as a specialist in the field of practice by: (A) the North Carolina State Bar; (B) an organization that is accredited by the North Carolina State Bar; or (C) an organization that is accredited by the American Bar Association under procedures and criteria endorsed by the North Carolina State Bar."

43. *Id.* at Comment 7.

44. *Id.* at Comment 8.

45. *See* Rule 4.-7.14 of the Florida State Bar, available at https://www-media.floridabar.org/uploads/2025/02/2025_06-DEC-RRTFB-12-30-2024-1.pdf (last visited Apr. 22, 2025).

focuses on, or limits the lawyer's practice to particular areas of practice as long as the statements are true."[46]

These examples are just a few of the significant variations from state to state on what language can be used in advertising specialization either with or without certification. Lawyers with a certification from a private entity (or seeking one) must therefore investigate whether the program is accredited by the ABA or approved by the state, and if so, what disclosures or disclaimers must accompany any communications to the public as to that certification. Lawyers without a certification but who specialize in a particular field must be careful to use only language permitted under state rules of professional responsibility, including avoiding the use of the word "specialist" or "specialize" depending on the jurisdiction.

Legal Specialization, Competence, and the Duty of Care

One of the concerns that has arisen with the proliferation of legal specialist certification programs is whether lawyers without such a certification satisfy their duty of "competence" toward their clients when taking a case in an area in which they specialize but lack certification. The general duty of competence—addressed in Rule 1.1 of the ABA Model Rules—ensures that general practitioners or specialists without a certification maintain the ability to take on cases.[47] As set forth in the comments to Rule 1.1, whether

46. *Id.* As another example of differences in approaches among the states, see Gary McNeil, *Ethical Considerations in Marketing and Advertising Specialization* (discussing applicable rules in Texas), available at https://www.americanbar.org/content/dam/aba/administrative/professional_responsibility/ethical_considerations_in_mktg_and_advertising_spz.pdf (last visited Apr. 22, 2025).

47. Rule 1.1: Competence, available at https://www.americanbar.org/groups/professional_responsibility/publications/model_rules_of_professional_conduct/rule_1_1_competence/ (last visited Apr. 22, 2025) ("A lawyer shall provide

a lawyer has the competence to take on a matter is determined on a case-by-case basis, looking to "the relative complexity and specialized nature of the matter, the lawyer's general experience, the lawyer's training and experience in the field in question, the preparation and study the lawyer is able to give the matter and whether it is feasible to refer the matter to, or associate or consult with, a lawyer of established competence in the field in question." For these reasons, a lawyer without certification as a specialist may continue to provide legal services so long as they comply with the general duties to ensure competence in the handling of the matter.[48]

Outside of ethical considerations, however, lawyers must always consider their duty of care in the context of potential legal malpractice claims. In general, a plaintiff claiming negligence by their attorney must plead and prove (1) the duty of care; (2) a breach of that duty; (3) the causal connection between the negligent conduct and the resulting injury; and (4) actual loss or damage.[49] Although the definition of the duty of care varies slightly from jurisdiction to jurisdiction in legal malpractice cases, in general terms, the duty of care requires that an attorney should exercise the skill and knowledge ordinarily possessed by attorneys under similar circumstances according to locality, custom, and special skills.[50]

---

competent representation to a client. Competent representation requires the legal knowledge, skill, thoroughness and preparation reasonably necessary for the representation.").

48. For example, as explained in the comments to Rule 1.1, a newly admitted lawyer may be able to handle a number of legal matters, but otherwise, a lawyer may be required to associate with a specialist or refer a matter in order to comply with the duty of competence.

49. Ronald Mallen, 2 Legal Malpractice § 20:4 (Thomson Reuters 2025 ed.).

50. *Id.* § 20:2; *see also* Herring, *supra* note 21, at 75 ("[I]n deciding whether or not an attorney's representation is competent, the court should look at the skills and knowledge possessed by attorneys of ordinary skill and capacity who are located in the same or similar locality under similar circumstances.").

With the advent of legal specialization certification programs in the 1970s and 1980s, and the ability of lawyers to hold themselves out as legal specialists following the Supreme Court's decisions in *Bates* and *Peel,* courts hearing legal malpractice cases began to confront the issue of whether there should be a heightened duty of care imposed on lawyers who hold themselves out as legal specialists.[51] California—one of the first states to offer legal specialist certification—led the way in recognizing a "specialist standard of care" in legal malpractice cases. In 1975, the California Court of Appeals held in *Wright v. Williams*[52] that a lawyer holding themself out "to the public and the profession as specializing in an area of the law must exercise the skill, prudence, and diligence exercised by other specialists of ordinary skill and capacity specializing in the same field."[53] As a collateral consequence of the recognition of a heightened duty of care for legal specialists, the California Court of Appeals also held that because the question of attorney negligence was a question of fact, the plaintiff was required to provide expert testimony (by a legal specialist in the area involved) as to the standard of care.[54]

Other jurisdictions followed California's lead in recognizing a heightened duty of care for legal specialists. For example, in *Duffey Law Office v. Tank Transportation,*[55] the Wisconsin Court of Appeals, noting that the law was becoming increasingly specialized, addressed the "pivotal issue" in a legal malpractice case of

---

51. *See* Herring, *supra* note 21, at 79–80.

52. 121 Cal. Rptr. 194 (Cal. Ct. App. 1975).

53. *Id.* at 199.

54. *Id.* As the court stated, "[W]ithout expert testimony that a reasonably prudent specialist in admiralty law would, under the facts as the trial court found them, have acted differently than did respondent, there is no basis to attach legal fault to his conduct." For more information on the use of experts to establish the standard of care, see Mallen, *supra* note 49, 4 Legal Malpractice § 37:131.

55. *Duffey Law Office, S.C. v. Tank Transp.*, 535 N.W.2d 91 (Wis. Ct. App. 1995).

whether "an attorney who represents to a client that the attorney has expertise greater than that of the average Wisconsin lawyer is to be held to a standard of professional care that is consistent with that claimed *expertise*."[56] The court concluded that "the answer to this question is 'yes.'"[57] Despite strict state rules that continued to restrict any representation of specialty outside of patent and admiralty, Duffey held himself out as an expert in the areas of labor law, collective bargaining agreements, and pension-fund contribution law. The court concluded that he "thus should be held to a standard of care that is consistent with that representation."[58] Other cases in the 1980s and 1990s reached similar conclusions.[59]

More recently, the D.C. Circuit in *Seed Co. v. Westerman*[60] applied a specialist standard of care in a legal malpractice action arising out of an unsuccessful application for a patent in which, as a result of counsel's noncompliance with Patent Office regulations, another inventor obtained the patent for the same invention. Relying on precedent from the District of Columbia courts, the court held that specialists must "adhere to a standard of conduct commensurate with" their "special training and experience."[61]

---

56. *Id.* at 92.

57. *Id.*

58. *Id.* at 93.

59. *See, e.g.*, *Rodriguez v. Horton*, 622 P.2d 261, 264 (N.M. Ct. App. 1980) ("A lawyer holding himself out to the public as specializing in an area of the law must exercise the same skill as other specialists of ordinary ability specializing in the same field."); *Rhodes v. Batilla*, 848 S.W.2d 833, 842–43 (Tex. Ct. App. 1993) (applying heightened standard of care to "one who holds himself out as an expert or specialist"); *Bent v. Green*, 466 A.2d 322, 325 (Conn. App. Ct. 1983) (an attorney has duty to exercise "the same degree of care, skill and diligence which other attorneys . . . in the same line of practice would have exercised in similar circumstances"); *Battle v. Thornton*, 646 A.2d 315, 323 (D.C. App. 1994) (recognizing heightened standard of care if the attorney "affirmatively represented" that they were a specialist).

60. 832 F.3d 325, 335 (D.C. Cir. 2016).

61. *Id.* at 337 (internal citations omitted).

This case law highlights some of the complicated issues that have arisen as a legal matter since legal certification and advertising specialist status have become more commonplace. As set forth in the case law, there may be a number of factors that determine whether a heightened duty of care will be applied in a legal malpractice case. First, there must be some representation of specialist status.[62] Holding a certification in a field would obviously satisfy this requirement, but for legal specialists without certification, the issue may depend on a more in-depth factual inquiry. Besides whether the attorney has held themself out as a specialist, the court may consider a number of issues,[63] including whether the field at issue is a recognized specialty—an issue that can be determined by whether the state or the ABA has recognized certification in that area.[64]

Ethical Issues Related to Obtaining and Maintaining Certified Specialist Status

When a lawyer determines that they wish to pursue certification as a legal specialist, there are additional ethical considerations that may arise during the process of obtaining and maintaining certification. First, during the application for certification, lawyers generally will have to take an exam, provide information to support the application, and submit references. These steps

62. *See, e.g.*, *Fishman v. Brooks*, 487 N.E.2d 1377, 1379 (Mass. 1986) ("An attorney who has not held himself out as a specialist owes his client a duty to exercise the degree of care and skill of an average qualified practitioner.").

63. *See* Herring, *supra* note 21, at 86 ("Generally, there are three issues that the court must decide before applying the higher standard of care required of specialists. First, is the field of law that is the subject of the dispute a specialty? Second, if the attorney erred in a specialty area, was the case complex enough to require a specialist? Third, if the answers to the first two issues are yes, will the court require expert witnesses and, if so, what will qualify one as an expert?").

64. *See id.*

in the process can raise a number of ethical concerns under the ABA Model Rules. Second, for judges who wish to maintain an existing certification after taking the bench or obtain a certification based on judicial service for use when returning to the bar, there are several issues to consider under the ABA *Model Code of Judicial Conduct.*

While there are no specific ethical rules under the ABA Model Rules with respect to obtaining certification as a specialist, lawyers have broad duties of integrity and honesty that apply whether seeking certification from a state bar or another entity. If a lawyer is applying to a state bar–sponsored certification program, the admitting authority's equivalent of Model Rule 8.1, Bar Admission and Disciplinary Matters, will apply. Model Rule 8.1 reads:

> An applicant for admission to the bar, or a lawyer in connection with a bar admission application or in connection with a disciplinary matter, shall not:
>
> (a) Knowingly make a false statement of material fact; or
>
> (b) Fail to disclose a fact necessary to correct a misapprehension known by the person to have arisen in the matter, or knowingly fail to respond to a lawful demand for information from an admissions or disciplinary authority, except that this rule does not require disclosure of information otherwise protected by Rule 1.6.

While this provision does not expressly apply to applicants for specialization status sponsored by a state bar, lawyers should proceed with the assumption that it does. Even if applying for certification by a private board, providing false or misleading information about the qualifications for specialization or other matters can rise to the level of professional misconduct. Under Model Rule 8.4(c), "It is professional misconduct for a lawyer to: engage in conduct involving dishonesty, fraud, deceit or misrepresentation."[65]

There are a number of scenarios during the application for certification in which a lawyer can run afoul of the applicable rules of professional conduct. For example, a lawyer must pay particularly careful attention to the details of their experience in the field of specialty and hours associated with practice in this area. One area of ethical peril under Rule 8.1 and Rule 8.4 is statements by the lawyer in their application with respect to the number of hours practiced in the specialized field (typically about 500 hours are required). Specialization committees will carefully vet for accuracy any information provided by the attorney on the specialization application to ensure, for example, that the applicant has the requisite number of hours practicing in the area of specialization. If a reviewing committee determines that the applicant misled the committee (for example, falsified or "puffed up" the hours), this could be very serious and have disciplinary consequences. Lawyers taking any specialization exam must also scrupulously avoid any concerns of cheating, including through the use of artificial intelligence (AI) to prepare responses. Exam reviewers are able to use software to detect cheating or unusual activity on any exam, and thus lawyers must be extremely careful to avoid even the appearance of improper exam responses.

Additionally, lawyers must adhere to the same standards of truthfulness and accuracy when soliciting references from peers and judges. For example, lawyers must avoid any statements or disclosures to peer references that could be considered dishonest or misleading, such as exaggerated statements about their time in the specialized field or other qualifications. When seeking references from judges, lawyers should also be mindful of several

---

65. Rule 8.4: Misconduct, available at https://www.americanbar.org/groups/professional_responsibility/publications/model_rules_of_professional_conduct/rule_8_4_misconduct/ (last visited Apr. 22, 2025).

additional considerations. First, if the lawyer makes a misrepresentation to the judge as to their qualifications, the judge may have a duty to inform the state bar's disciplinary authorities. As set forth in Rule 2.15(B) of the ABA *Model Code of Judicial Conduct*:

> A judge having knowledge that a lawyer has committed a violation of the Rules of Professional Conduct that raises a substantial question regarding the lawyer's honesty, trustworthiness, or fitness as a lawyer in other respects shall inform the appropriate authority.[66]

Second, judges may be hesitant to provide a reference given the restriction on use of the prestige of the judicial office to advance the private interests of others in Rule 1.3 of the *Model Code of Judicial Conduct*[67] and the restriction on providing character testimony on behalf of others under Model Rule 3.3.[68] Although the *Model Code of Judicial Conduct* does not address the issue of references for certification as a specialist, a number of states have issued advisory opinions permitting judges to do so. As set forth in one compilation by the American Judicature Society, a number of judicial ethics advisory committees have issued opinions that a judge may provide a reference for an attorney in connection with certification as a specialist in an area of law, as

---

66. Rule 2.15: Responding to Judicial and Lawyer Misconduct, available at https://www.americanbar.org/groups/professional_responsibility/publications/model_code_of_judicial_conduct/model_code_of_judicial_conduct_canon_2/rule2_15respondingtojudicialandlawyermisconduct/ (last visited Apr. 22, 2025).

67. Rule 1.3: Avoiding Abuse of the Prestige of Judicial Office, available at https://www.americanbar.org/groups/professional_responsibility/publications/model_code_of_judicial_conduct/mcjc_canon_1/rule1_3avoidingabuseoftheprestigeofthejudicialoffice/ (last visited Apr. 22, 2025).

68. Rule 3.3: Testifying as a Character Witness, available at https://www.americanbar.org/groups/professional_responsibility/publications/model_code_of_judicial_conduct/model_code_of_judicial_conduct_canon_3/rule3_3testifyingasacharterwitness/ (last visited Apr. 22, 2025).

long as the reference is confidential, even if the attorney has a case pending before the judge.[69] A lawyer requesting such a reference, or a judge who receives such a request, should consult with their judicial ethics advisory body to determine if there is a published formal advisory opinion on this issue or, if not, whether confidential informal advice can be given before completing the reference form.

There are several other issues with respect to judges and legal specialization that bear caution as well. For example, new judges coming to the bench with a certification as a specialist may wish to retain that status after assuming the bench. Certification as a legal specialist needs to be maintained through continued practice in the specialty area. Once on the bench, however, judges may be prohibited from practicing law.[70] New judges who wish to retain their status should consult with their regulatory authority to inquire if there is a judicial inactive certification that will allow the judge to maintain certification while in judicial service. Even so, the judge may have to show that they hear cases in the area of specialty in order to maintain their status while on the bench. For example, appellate judges may be able to maintain appellate

69. *See* Cynthia Gray, Recommendations by Judges, American Judicature Society (2009), available at https://www.ncsc.org/__data/assets/pdf_file/0028/17398/recommendationsbyjudges.pdf (last visited Apr. 22, 2025) (citing Arizona Advisory Opinion 02-4, Florida Advisory Opinion 78-24, Nebraska Advisory Opinion 94-2, New Jersey Guidelines on Extrajudicial Activities Addendum A, New York Advisory Opinion 93-129, Ohio Advisory Opinion 98-4). *But see* New Jersey Advisory Opinions 16-01 and 3-06 (judge should not fill out a questionnaire from the American Academy of Matrimonial Lawyers seeking information regarding an applicant for a fellowship); South Carolina Advisory Opinion 26-2006 (judge may not submit a form reference for an attorney to the American Board of Professional Liability Lawyers).

70. *See, e.g.*, Model Code of Judicial Conduct Rule 3.10, available at https://www.americanbar.org/groups/professional_responsibility/publications/model_code_of_judicial_conduct/model_code_of_judicial_conduct_canon_3/rule3_10practiceoflaw/ (last visited Apr. 22, 2025).

specialization status because they hear only appellate cases, or family court judges may be able to retain their certification in family law. Again, this is an issue specific to each jurisdiction that requires the judge to contact their regulatory agency regarding whether any accommodation for judges is permitted.

Finally, there may also be situations in which a judge—in preparing to leave the bench—may wish to seek specialization status. A judge should consider waiting until after stepping down from the bench to complete the application, primarily because the peer reference process may require a judge to seek references from attorneys who appear before them, thus creating a conflict of interest that may lead to disqualification issues. In addition, judges must comply with the same processes for application as lawyers, including demonstrating the requisite hours of practice in the specialty area. Again, this can present difficulties because judges may be prohibited from practicing law and thus may struggle to establish hours in practice necessary for specialization status. Some states, however, may allow judges to use time on the bench in specialty courts as a substitute for practice of law. For this reason, a judge wishing to obtain certification as a legal specialist should consult with their state bar for specific details on whether such credit for judicial service is available.

Conclusion

The evolution of the practice of law in the last 50 years has been marked by the freedom of lawyers to advertise a legal specialty and the advent of certification programs for legal specialists. Both of these developments have raised a number of ethical issues for lawyers to consider. Although the ABA Model Rules of Professional Conduct have few specific rules on the issue of certification (and even then are limited to the issue of advertising), lawyers must always consider their broader duties to provide competent representation, avoid any conduct or statements that could be considered false or misleading, and be mindful of interactions with judges during the application process. For judges who wish to retain their specialization certification while on the bench or gain it before departing the bench, additional considerations come into play under the ABA *Model Code of Judicial Conduct*. For such judges, their desire to have certification must yield to the paramount duty to maintain public confidence in the integrity, impartiality, and independence of the judiciary. All is not lost for such judges, however, as state bars continue to consider mechanisms for judges to meet and maintain their qualifications as legal specialists.

Chapter 5

Blazing a Trail: Musings on Creation of a New Certified Legal Specialty

Grant B. Osborne

> "Some men see things as they are, and say why. I dream things that never were, and say why not."
>
> —George Bernard Shaw

Introduction

This is a brief chapter about what it takes to try to create or, more accurately, help others to try to create a new certified specialty in the practice of law.

That practice, as all lawyers know—or should know—is a privilege that is granted and highly regulated by each of the several states. The states do that because we lawyers are in a position to do enormous good—or enormous harm—because we, far more than nonlawyers, know the rules by which we all live in civil society. Everyone is required to live by them, but only lawyers have a good handle on what the most important of them actually are (or at least have easy access to them). The philosopher Jerry Seinfeld once put it well: "What are lawyers, really? To me, a lawyer is basically the person that knows the rules of the country. We're all throwing the dice, playing the game, moving our pieces around the board, but if there's a problem, the lawyer is the only person that has read the inside of the top of the box."

Indeed we have. And that expertise comes with a heavy responsibility—that of identifying and promoting, competently and honestly, the best interests of our clients.

The agencies that regulate lawyers' conduct have an equally significant responsibility—that of ensuring that lawyers are at least minimally competent in the fields in which they represent clients and purport to know what they're doing. But here's the problem: a license to practice law is, by definition, a license to practice law *generally*. In the author's home state of North Carolina (and presumably in all other jurisdictions), the state regulatory agency (in North Carolina, the North Carolina State Bar) has never required a licensee to prove competence in a *particular* legal field. One is required, rather, to demonstrate competence in the law *generally* (and, for that matter, only *once*, usually on the heels of completion of law school). One could argue, and many have, that satisfaction of such a generic and singular requirement does little to inform the public about whether a particular lawyer in a particular field is proficient in it.

The notion that an attorney could not only hold a law license but also be recognized by a regulatory authority as proficient in a particular field is relatively new. But many regulatory agencies, and lawyers themselves, have come to recognize that demonstrations of such objective proficiency provide a valuable tool to the consuming public in their quest to find lawyers who are well equipped to serve their needs.

For all that, the certification of proficiency of lawyers in various fields is still relatively rare; relatively few practicing lawyers are certified in anything. But the idea that lawyers should have the *opportunity* to become certified in recognized legal fields has now taken root.

That's happened for two primary reasons. First, state agencies that regulate lawyers recognize that such certifications *promote the public interest*—specifically, clients' interest in identifying lawyers with the kinds of subject-matter proficiency and skills that they need. Second, lawyers themselves recognize that such certifications provide them with an opportunity to demonstrate their competence objectively and thus promote their services to potential clients.

There are many legal fields in which various states issue certifications of proficiency, such as real estate, tax, appellate practice, bankruptcy, family law, immigration, and intellectual property. But that's a distinct subset of all discrete fields in which lawyers *might* be certified (of which there are probably dozens).

That presents an opportunity. Lawyers in many states may conclude that certifications in many fields of practice that don't yet exist should be adopted. Such lawyers may believe that "someone should do something" to bring that about. But we all know that nothing happens unless someone takes the first step. This writer, for example, *with the dedicated involvement and assistance of many others*, did that, for the purpose of persuading the North Carolina State Bar to recognize a certified specialty in employment law. The specialty was approved by the North Carolina Supreme Court on March 20, 2024.[1]

This writer has thus been asked to provide a few thoughts about what that experience entailed, in the hope of providing guidance to others who may wish to chart a similar path in their own jurisdictions with respect to fields of their choice.

---

1. The writer would like to extend special thanks to two attorneys who helped to spearhead that effort: **William Oden** (also of Ward and Smith, P.A.), of Wilmington, N.C., and **Phillip Gibbons**, of Charlotte, N.C. The writer is also grateful to **Denise Mullen**, M.Ed., Ed.D., former Managing Director, Board of Legal Specialization of the North Carolina State Bar, who patiently guided us through the thicket of rules and procedures that preceded creation of the specialty. Without her help, it wouldn't have gotten off the ground.

Why Do Legal Specializations Exist? Should There Be Another One?

The practice of law, in the United States anyway, consists of a dizzying array of legal subjects, skills, and arts. One can be a highly skilled practitioner in fields such as antitrust, bankruptcy, or criminal law but know little about the law of damages, elder law, or family law—to say nothing of subjects beyond the letter F. For that matter, one may be a highly skilled trial lawyer but be lost at sea when it comes to appellate practice, in which there are too many shoals to count. A student can graduate from a law school, pass a bar exam, and obtain a license to practice law and then be free, as far as regulatory authorities are concerned, to practice law in almost any field in which the budding lawyer hopes to succeed.

But anyone who has practiced law for more than a few years—and perhaps anyone who has done so at all—knows that mere *entitlement* to practice law equips one not at all to provide a client with *competent* legal advice and representation. That kind of competence, in any field of practice, requires years of additional study and experience. Both are essential before any lawyer, regardless of intelligence, common sense, character, or credential, can hope to provide real value to a client unless doing so under the watchful eye of a more experienced practitioner.

Does the consuming public always know that? Almost certainly not. Look at or listen to the ubiquitous marketing efforts that lawyers publish to promote themselves online, on television and radio, on billboards, in newspapers and magazines, and on buses and at bus stops. You may be impressed. You may see a lot of information about the size of verdicts and settlements that have purportedly been won or secured; the lawyer's peerless enthusiasm for his or her clients' needs; and third-party rankings (often cultivated) of lawyers and their firms. But, for all of that subjective promotion, you'll rarely see any representation about the *objective proficiency* of the attorneys in question.

That's because, before the era of legal specialization, few if any criteria on that subject existed. The consuming public is familiar with specialists in disciplines of all kinds, the most obvious of which are medicine and allied fields—think allergists, cardiologists, gastroenterologists, and X-ray technologists, to name a few. There are specialists in other industries too, such as construction (roofers, electricians, and plumbers), finance (commercial lenders and investment advisors), and information technology (programmers and network managers).

But before regulatory agencies and courts began to create certified legal specialties, the consuming public had no *objective* way of knowing whether an attorney who practices in a particular field was any good at it. Sure, there have always been meaningful *subjective* criteria that one may consult to try to determine whether a particular attorney is highly skilled. One of the most reliable has always been—and will continue to be—the lawyer's reputation among lawyers and others who have worked with that lawyer. One assumes, for example, that reputation alone, among lawyers and nonlawyers, was a reliable indication of the competence of legal luminaries such as John Adams, Abraham Lincoln, and Ruth Bader Ginsberg; no one needed an objective standard to feel confident that they were (to say the least) good lawyers.

That's true for outliers of unusual smarts and skill. But, when it comes to the rest of us, reference to *objective* criteria can only help. One would be hard pressed to think of a reason why reference to such criteria would not be helpful in determining whether a particular lawyer is adequately skilled in a particular field. Why? For the simple reason described earlier—it's perfectly legal for lawyers, in any state of the union, to offer up their services in a legal field or discipline without first having proven to anyone that they are competent in it.

That arresting notion should give you pause. There's nothing in my home state of North Carolina, for example, to prevent me from offering my services in the fields of criminal defense, trusts and estates, or corporate mergers and acquisitions—although I have no skill or experience *in any of them*. Sure, if I were to do so (and get a client to hire me), then I might get sued for professional malpractice or be disciplined (and perhaps disbarred) by the North Carolina State Bar. But I might not. And, even if I were, then that may happen long after I've led an unsuspecting client into an avoidable conviction, boneheaded will, or stupid merger agreement.

Can anything be done to help the public avoid such disastrous consequences? You bet. The answer is to offer *certification of legal specialization* in fields of practice that are discrete enough to warrant wide acknowledgment that they exist and be susceptible to reliable objective testing of practitioners' proficiency.

Many such specializations may already exist in your state. In North Carolina, the North Carolina State Bar has certified practitioners in many fields, such as appellate practice, bankruptcy law, elder law, family law, immigration law, and workers' compensation law (among many others). The State Bar has been doing so since 1987—so this is nothing new.

You may look at the certified specialties in your state and believe that there should, perhaps, be another one in a recognized field, because clients who need lawyers in that field lack a reliable way of assessing the *objective proficiency* of those who claim to practice it. *Objective* proficiency is almost never, by itself, an adequate indication of competence. There are many *subjective* criteria that may and *should* be considered by a client when deciding whether to hire a lawyer—such as the attorney's ability to build rapport and trust with the client, his or her apparent competence in the field, whether he or she has been recommended by someone whom the prospective client trusts, and, in some cases, the apparent resources of the law firm of which the attorney is a part. But the availability of such subjective criteria is not an argument that *objective* criteria have no place in the equation.

If objective criteria that can be used to evaluate proficiency in a particular field do not yet exist, then perhaps someone should look into trying to bring them about. That's a worthy goal, because the effort may lead to helping clients who need lawyers in that field make informed decisions about whom to hire when they need assistance with what are often significant and sometimes life-changing problems.

If so, then perhaps that someone should be you. Why not?

Now That You've Decided to Do It, What Next?

Don't Go It Alone

Identify one or two others who share your vision, who are willing and able to help, and who will hold you accountable

Change is hard. People, especially lawyers, are creatures of habit. Lawyers like to navigate familiar rules, so many lawyers find it disquieting when someone suggests that some of the rules by which they practice their livelihoods should be changed. Proposing that a certified specialty should be recognized for the first time—even when no one is *required* to be certified—can be daunting.

That's a good reason not to undertake that task alone. You should give serious consideration to enlisting the help of one, two, or three other people—but probably not more than that—to form an initial committee for the purpose of shepherding a proposed certification from concept to fact. Others whom you enlist may have valuable ideas about how to approach the task in ways of which you hadn't thought, and your committee can help to share what will undoubtedly be more work than you had contemplated. Members of the committee can also help to hold one another accountable for the completion of assigned tasks and thus help to ensure that, in the midst of busy lives and careers, the goal doesn't get stuck in the mud or, worse, abandoned.

Identify and Master the Applicable Rules

Unless your state has never certified lawyers in any field, you are not the first to undertake the task. Your jurisdiction almost certainly has rules of some kind that prescribe the way in which a new certification can be developed. One of your first jobs, therefore, is to identify the rules and read them thoroughly, so that you will have at least a rudimentary understanding of the rules of the road on which you are about to embark. (Let's call them the "Development Rules.")

Determine Who Must Be Involved

States that certify lawyers in specialties of various kinds have almost certainly appointed officers of a court or state regulatory agency who have been tasked with assisting with the development of a new specialty. One of your first jobs, therefore, is to learn who they are and get to know them. You may find that they are among your most ardent cheerleaders and may be eager to walk with you down the road toward creation of the new specialty. They can also familiarize you with the nuances, practicalities, and administrative steps inherent in the Development Rules that may not be apparent from the rules themselves. You should cultivate your relationships with all of them. They may prove to be of enormous assistance.

Determine Who Should Be Involved—Relationships Matter

You may find that there are many groups (such as mandatory or voluntary bar associations) and individuals in your state who have—or claim to have—a stake or interest in the creation of, or opposition to, a new specialty. The Development Rules may not indicate that such a stake or interest exists. That may be beside the point.

You should go out of your way to solicit their thoughts and opinions. Why? Because politics is the art of the possible, and an effort to change the law in your state regarding creation of a proposed legal specialty is inherently political. You should therefore invite and give serious consideration to the thoughts and opinions of those who have an interest in the new idea, for at least two reasons. *First, you should give them an opportunity to be heard,* in addition to the opportunity that may be prescribed by law, if only to ensure that your work is transparent and fair. Great things, as Tolstoy said, often happen in slow and inconspicuous ways, but little of lasting value is done surreptitiously. *Second, you should make every effort to learn and understand all competing arguments.* The various regulatory authorities who will consider your idea will almost certainly hear them at some point. The prudent advocate will scout out and consider the opposition at the earliest opportunity.

Develop a Plan for Success So That You Can Know Whether You're, Well, Succeeding

The Development Rules in your jurisdiction almost certainly prescribe the steps that will need to be accomplished for the proposed specialty to be brought to fruition. You should develop a detailed outline of what those steps are and of (at least) an aspirational timeline in accordance with which you hope to accomplish them.

What gets measured gets done. A detailed outline, crafted and adopted by members of your initial development committee, will provide an invaluable tool for identifying and measuring the accomplishment of milestones along the way. "A goal without a plan is just a wish" (Antoine de Saint-Exupéry), so you need a plan; your outline will be that plan. But it must be a living document—amend it from time to time in accordance with new information and consult it regularly to document what you have accomplished and, just as important, what remains to be done.

Essential Features of Success (and How to Avoid Messing Things Up)

Build Alliances

The undertaking on which you're about to embark should not be done alone. Identify those who may be willing to help you. You'll probably find that many are and have simply been waiting for someone to take the lead. But be humble about the effort and remember that it isn't about you—*it's about what's good for the public*. Keep that in mind and work toward developing a winning team with that prime directive in mind and you'll be far more likely to succeed.

Keep Your Friends Close—and Your Enemies Closer

You will almost certainly have no true "enemies" in your effort, but you may encounter principled opposition. If you hope to succeed, then you will respect the opposition and give serious consideration to their arguments, some of which you may find you haven't considered. Remember that, "[w]hen you know how to listen, everybody is the guru" (Ram Dass). So listen up. What you learn will probably be of real value.

Moreover, keep in mind that even your opponents are likely to be fellow members of the bar with whom you'll need and want to work productively in coming years, for the sake of your clients and professional collegiality. You'll do yourself, your clients, and your effort a real disservice if you burn bridges along the way.

The best way to avoid doing that is to take nothing about the opposition personally. If people are opposing your effort and lodging arguments against it, then they're almost certainly doing so for reasons that, again, *have nothing to do with you*. They may stem, rather, from worries and concerns about how their lives and work may be affected by the proposed specialty. Keep those concerns in mind, respect them, and try to identify arguments that may help to persuade your opponents that their fears are misplaced or at least exaggerated. You may find, if you have been respectful, that some of your opponents may become, if not your advocates, then at least neutral observers.

That was my experience. In my and others' work on development of a new certified specialty in North Carolina, we encountered zealous opposition—even though the proposed specialty never contemplated that anyone would be *required* to become certified in it to practice in the field. Certification in the proposed specialty, in other words, was always intended to be and promoted as *optional*; a lawyer might *choose* to become certified, but no one suggested that he or she *must* do so.

One might then wonder why there was opposition at all. In our case, the opponents offered up various reasons, such as (in no particular order):

- The proposed specialty isn't needed by the public to help prospective clients identify good employment lawyers, because adequate means of doing that already exist.
- Existence of the proposed specialty, even if optional, will create an unfair commercial advantage for some lawyers (e.g., those who choose to become certified) at the expense of others (e.g., those who don't).
- The proposed specialty will be unfair because it will be easier for management-side lawyers to become and remain certified than for employee-side lawyers to do so (because

of certification and mandatory CLE-related fees that may be more affordable for some than others, and because of the perception that management-side lawyers' practices may give them a leg up when it comes to performing well on the specialty examination).

- The proposed specialty will harm consumers because it will lead to an increase in fees that can be charged by certified lawyers.
- The proposed specialty will give an unfair advantage to certified lawyers because judges before whom cases are litigated will have more confidence in their arguments than in those of noncertified lawyers.
- "If it ain't broke, don't fix it": The employment bar has gotten along fine without the specialty for decades. There's no need to create one now.
- The executive leadership of the voluntary bar association of employment lawyers is unwilling to endorse creation of the specialty. The State Bar, in the absence of such an endorsement, should therefore refrain from creating it.

Such arguments were presented in various ways to the North Carolina State Bar at various steps along the way. But none got traction, despite being eloquently advanced by experienced and highly reputable lawyers. Why?

Because none of them struck at the heart of the matter, which is this: Will the proposed specialty serve the interests of the public by providing consumers of legal services with another useful way of identifying lawyers who are equipped, by skill and experience, to serve their needs? The answer to that was—and is—an unequivocal yes, regardless of arguments to the contrary.

That's not to say that such arguments were, or should have been, casually dismissed. They were not. Each was confronted head-on, with respect for those who advanced it. That approach led to a principled debate about the merits of the proposed specialty in which reason rather than fear prevailed. It also led to productive working relationships with members of the opposition, some of whom later agreed to participate in development of the specialty examination. That they did so demonstrates the value of, again, not taking opposition personally. You'll find that surprisingly easy if you keep your eye on the ball.

See the Plan Through

Let's not kid ourselves. Few careers are as stressful as the practice of law. A busy practice can be overwhelming and make it hard for lawyers to accomplish tasks that have nothing directly to do with securing, retaining, and communicating with clients, complying with deadlines of various kinds, and paying the bills. Adding to that an effort to try to change the law in your jurisdiction by creating a new certified specialty can be, to say the least, optimistic.

But, once you have made the commitment to try to accomplish the goal, you must reserve time in your schedule on a weekly and monthly basis to see the task through. Be realistic about what you can hope to accomplish but hold yourself and your colleagues accountable for the accomplishment of identified tasks. Divide the effort into its constituent parts, and you'll find that accomplishment of each of them, one by one, isn't as difficult as perhaps you'd imagined. And keep in mind that, as Theodore Roosevelt said, "Far and away the best prize that life has to offer is the chance to work hard at work worth doing." The work of trying to create an objectively based certified legal specialty that clients can consider when trying to find lawyers who can help them is certainly that.

Keep Your Eye on the Ball

The ball, in this case, is the *public's interest* in access to an *objective* indication of a lawyer's proficiency in a field of practice in which the lawyer wishes to earn clients' trust. It is nothing less than that. If you keep that in mind amid the inevitable untidiness and surprises that accompany any tough slog, then you are likely to succeed.

Chapter 6

Appellate Specialization

Troy D. Shelton

Are you thinking about pursuing legal specialization but not sure if it's worth it? You're not alone. Specialization is a big step and usually requires a substantial investment.

But you are ultimately investing in yourself. I pursued specialization and happily vouch for it. The return on your investment will be both internal—a greater sense of confidence—and external for those who want to market their services in private practice.

Why Seek Specialization?

It's probably no surprise to you that the legal field has become increasingly specialized. Though some attorneys bemoan that change, the trend shows no signs of reversing.

Many attorneys like the benefits that flow from specialization. Rather than constantly learning something new, a specialist can become a subject-matter expert. Attorneys who have mastered their craft are naturally more confident at work. That, in turn, tends to increase job satisfaction, which is important in a profession that often leads to burnout.

For some attorneys, this internal motivation is reason enough to seek a specialist's certificate. They want to prove to themselves and the world that they are, in fact, masters at their craft. Besides, many attorneys like the intellectual stimulation that comes from focusing on one area of the law.

For others, especially lawyers in private practice, the rewards of specialization can also be external. For starters, specialists usually command higher rates. Plus, it's a lot easier to build a reputation when you specialize. Specialization helps both prospective clients and referral sources recognize that you don't just dabble in a practice area. It's easy to say, for instance, that you "handle appeals." It means something else entirely when the state bar says that you're a board-certified specialist.

And that's how I hold myself out. In 2022, I became board certified as an appellate specialist in North Carolina. At the time, I worked at an AmLaw 100 law firm, with the biggest appellate team in the state. Besides those reasons just noted, specialization was important to me for some additional reasons.

First and foremost, my age. When I took the exam, I was eight years out of law school. There were no other appellate specialists as young as me. Although I had just made partner at my firm, I saw specialization as an important way to make myself marketable to clients, my relative youth notwithstanding. Clients and referral sources want to know that I'm experienced enough to deserve their trust. Being a board-certified appellate specialist was a valuable way to prove it.

Second, there was a good kind of unspoken peer pressure from my appellate colleagues. It was something that my team expected, since all of us were focusing our work on appeals, and all the attorneys senior to me were already board-certified appellate specialists. We often spoke about what steps were needed to get me prepared for specialization. It never occurred to me that I *wouldn't* seek specialization, given how our team worked. And I'm glad for it.

Perhaps you're even earlier in the specialization process: you've dipped your toes in the water, and like it, but aren't sure whether you want to take the deep dive of specialization. To further test the waters, a good next step is getting involved in your state bar association if it has a section in your potential specialty. Reach out to the section head and ask what you can do to get involved. I got involved in my state's appellate section before I was even aware that specialization existed. I made great connections and friends.

Am I Eligible to Specialize?

When many think of legal specialization, their minds head directly to the exam. The exam is important, but specialization is a play in two parts. The exam comes second, but what's more important is becoming eligible to sit for the exam.

Eligibility requirements vary by state and specialty. But they are generally focused on one thing: proving that you are *already* devoted to the specialty. You do not wake up one day and decide that you'll be a bankruptcy specialist. It's not enough to have practiced criminal law for a couple of years. Becoming a real expert takes time. The expert needs to have devoted enough time to the specialty to have tackled a wide variety of problems for their clients. In other words, to become a specialist, you really should already be a specialist.

Getting to eligibility takes planning, at least for many specialties. Take my appellate specialty, which is what I know best. Among other requirements, the prospective specialist must average 400 hours per year—over five years—on appeals. This means that an attorney is devoting 20 to 25 percent of his or her practice to appeals for half a decade.

Appellate work doesn't just fall out of the sky, and there aren't a lot of jobs that can help an attorney get that much appellate work. An attorney seeking specialization may seek a position as part of an established appellate team in a law firm, which is what I did. But government jobs can provide similar, if not greater, experience in a specialty. Attorneys in government positions—even young attorneys—can often get a great depth of experience in a specialty in a short time. And, given government constraints, young attorneys are often put in charge of their own cases. That's not an experience that private practice can match. Although it can sometimes feel like a trial by fire, the lessons learned can be invaluable.

To get your specialization while in private practice, you may need to work for free or at a reduced rate. My specialty required a minimum of five appellate oral arguments, but those are hard to come by, even when working on an appellate team in a law firm. Clients and other pressures usually make the senior partner the face of the appeal, especially at oral argument.

Pro bono work helped me get my arguments quickly. I was already a big proponent of pro bono work. I helped to create North Carolina's appellate pro bono program. When I set my sights on appellate specialization, I simply redirected my pro bono efforts into work for indigent clients on appellate cases. If you're a young attorney that's still seeking to meet the eligibility requirement, I highly recommend looking into pro bono work to accelerate your efforts.

That's doubly true if your employer will support it. My colleagues were very helpful in taking cases pro bono or at extremely reduced rates so that I could be lead counsel.

Your colleagues are important resources in getting eligibility. If you want to specialize, make your wishes known to them. Let them know what requirements you need, and ask if they have any ideas to help you. That's true even if your colleagues aren't specialists or focus on some other kind of law. I have a friend who wanted to focus on appeals. Because she made her wishes known, the other litigators in the firm could funnel appeals her way. But that can't happen if you keep your specialization interest a secret.

What's the Specialization Exam Like?

I recommend that you take the preparation seriously. Maybe not quite like studying for the bar exam, but don't assume it will be a cakewalk either. In the year that I sat for the appellate exam, five of us sat for the exam. Only two of us passed.

A well-designed specialization exam will imitate the practice of the specialty itself. It should (and in my experience did) test the types of problems that consistently arise in the practice area. If you are well rounded in the specialty area, then the exam and preparation should look a lot like what you're already doing.

That said, hopefully you can spot some of the gaps in your experience and knowledge. Even if you've kept at it for the past several years, there are probably some rabbit holes that you haven't fully explored or encountered at all. Admit where those gaps are and make a plan to bridge them.

If you can, talk to attorneys who have recently passed the exam. They probably can't talk specifics, but they may be happy to share study tips, including both general study techniques and particular topics worthy of your attention.

Sometimes practitioners have a niche within a niche, such as a lawyer who focuses on just criminal appeals instead of civil and criminal appeals. If you know that's you, then your prep may need to be more extensive than others. Talk to specialists who do what you don't. What kinds of issues would they expect to see tested on the exam? And what resources would they recommend for you to learn how to handle this other kind of work?

The format of specialization exams varies by state and specialty, but the format should inform how you study. Is the exam made up of multiple-choice questions, essay questions, or both? Are you allowed to use any materials (like rule books) or notes?

You probably aren't interested in the specifics of appellate specialization in North Carolina, but maybe it would be of some help for me to share how I prepared. I knew the exam was a half day of multiple-choice and essay questions, modeled on the bar exam. (The other half of the exam was a weeklong, take-home exercise that involved editing and writing.) I read all the materials recommended by the exam committee. In part, that meant spending my evenings slowly reading through the Rules of Appellate Procedure, state and federal, and tracking down issues that I hadn't considered before.

I wasn't trying to memorize the rules, since the exam allowed me to use the rule books and relevant statutes. But I wanted to know where I could turn in the rules to figure out the questions on the multiple-choice part of the exam. When I took the exam, I forced myself to look up each rule or statute that governed so that I could be extra sure of my answer. I didn't trust my intuition on the exam, just like I don't do that for clients on important issues.

I also knew that the essay part of the exam would take a deep dive on issues that weren't necessarily contained in the rules themselves. To prepare for this part of the exam, I flipped through our state's (rather lengthy) appellate treatise. I focused on several chapters that I thought would make good test subjects and where my knowledge was potentially lacking.

In Retrospect, Was It Worth It?

Without a doubt. I left my big law job behind in 2024 and moved to "small law" with two other attorneys, neither of whom focus on appeals. If I hadn't gotten my specialization, I'm not sure that the move would have been a wise choice. Having the specialization credential is important when prospective clients and referring lawyers consider whether to send me work. It creates a baseline of trust because the state bar is vouching for my expertise. And because I'm still a relatively young lawyer and expanding my network of referral sources, that trust is invaluable.

If you get specialized and want to use the specialization for marketing, consider ways to build on the credential with other marketing efforts. You could start a blog, run an email newsletter, or put on continuing education programs for nonexperts.

Don't discount the importance of nonspecialist attorneys. If you're in private practice, nonspecialists are a critical source of referral business. Find ways to help the nonspecialists with your expertise, and you may receive referrals in return.

* * *

If you are already inclined to focus on a particular area of the law, I strongly recommend that you give legal specialization some thought. Specialization can help you craft a fulfilling legal career. Although it takes some patience and persistence, the rewards are well worth it.

Index